LONGWOOD GARDENS

100+ YEARS *of* GARDEN SPLENDOR

LONGWOOD GARDENS

100+ YEARS *of* GARDEN SPLENDOR

COLVIN RANDALL

THIRD EDITION

Contents

COVER: Conservatory Orangery during Orchid Extravaganza, 2018; PAGE 1: Acacia in Orangery lawn, c. 1947; PAGE 2: Exhibition Hall, c. 1947; LEFT: Flowering cherries, 2004

Nathan Hayward, III, (left) with his sister Nancy Lloyd Hayward and their great-uncle Pierre S. du Pont at Longwood, 1946.

Foreword

Pierre du Pont's papers bear no mention of his ever having met J. M. Barrie, Lewis Carroll, or L. Frank Baum. But I have to believe they would have thoroughly enjoyed each other's company. Just think of Wendy and the Lost Boys, Alice and her entourage, or Dorothy, the Scarecrow, Tin Man plus the Cowardly Lion transported to Kennett Square. They'd certainly have found the 20th-century equivalents of Neverland, the Rabbit Hole, and the Yellow Brick Road somewhere within these enchanted acres! Pierre undoubtedly would have found something in common with each of these three men. All four came from very large families of nine or more children. Barrie was an ardent spokesman for conservation in his native Scotland. Carroll was an Oxford mathematician and a serious published academic long before the Mad Hatter and the March Hare became well-beloved public figures. Baum, like Pierre, was a sickly child whose father became a successful industrialist.

But I'll bet that most annealing would have been their love for children. The literary legacies that the three authors left us have become treasured experiences for children and parents around the world. Less well known, but very much a part of Pierre's more private side, was his uncanny appreciation for the fantasies, and mischief, of the young. This enduring affection was as much a part of his character as his public persona—the truly creative management genius, his engineering inquisitiveness, determined civic leadership, and his passion for plants, music, and the theater. He had no children of his own; he and his first cousin Alice Belin, who had been friends for many years, were married after her childbearing years. But Pierre was a devoted uncle to more than three-dozen nieces and nephews. He became legal guardian to three of them when his younger brother, William K., died at 32, leaving them fatherless at very young ages. He was a generous friend to countless other cousins and in-laws, and a true father figure to the extended families of Longwood's staff, many of whom represented the third or fourth generation to have worked the land and cared for the arboretum in Peirce's Park. Throughout his life, Pierre always found time in his busy schedule to get inside young minds and delight in their never-ending imaginations. He was a practical joker, a source of constant amusement, a gentle disciplinarian, or a shoulder for a boy or girl to cry on when their parents didn't seem to understand.

I was one of the luckiest of his extended family because my own parents brought me and my two sisters to live with my great Uncle for seven months while our newly purchased house was being renovated. Memories of those days endure as though they happened only last week. An early breakfast with our host, who always insisted that it was the best meal of the day and should be shared by everyone. A ride on the Longwood fire engine for my third birthday party. My flooding the guest bathroom after depositing a large cake of soap in the flushometer toilet; it took Uncle Pierre and a makeshift screwdriver (a dime) to stop the cascade. These happy encounters continued until his death in 1954. We'd often go for Sunday afternoon visits in the garden, to feed the ducks and play make

believe on the outdoor stage. In bad weather, we'd gather in his living room where my parents would work with him on picture puzzles, and we kids would play with the wonderful stash of toys which were carefully stored in the large bottom drawer of his specially designed map files.

Today [2005], more than half a century later, I have the equal good luck to be serving as President of Longwood's Board of Trustees. As I think back on what this treasured oasis has meant to me and millions of other visitors, I am convinced that Pierre must have read one of Barrie's papers delivered to an audience in St. Andrews, Scotland, in 1922. "God gave us memories so that we might have roses in December," Barrie wrote. Perhaps this was an unwitting challenge to Pierre's ambition to make Longwood a haven where people could actually come to see and smell those roses every day throughout the year. From my childhood infatuation with topiary and colored fountains, to my present day commitment to help preserve and enhance this incredible gift, I think how fortunate we are to live within the arc of Longwood's magic. Although this book celebrates the Gardens' first hundred years, it is really dedicated to the hope that the next century of children, and their parents, will continue to delight in the youthful joys and adult reveries of this most special of places.

Nathan Hayward, III
President, Board of Trustees, 2003-2015
Trustee Emeritus, 2015

Introduction

Exquisite flowers, majestic trees, dazzling fountains, opulent conservatory, starlit theatre, thunderous organ—all describe the magic of Longwood Gardens, a horticultural showstopper where the gardening arts are encased in classic forms but enhanced by cyber-age technology. For 100 years, Longwood has flourished in ways that are highly visible, yet in others are virtually unseen. As we celebrate a century of many achievements, it is important to realize that Longwood's past was, and hopefully its future will be, shaped by the remarkable vision and versatility of one of the 20th century's most extraordinary men.

Pierre S. du Pont (1870-1954)—industrialist, conservationist, farmer, designer, engineer, impresario, and philanthropist—was the great-grandson of Eleuthère Irénée du Pont (1771-1834), who arrived from France in 1800 and founded the DuPont gunpowder company two years later. Pierre turned the family business into a corporate empire and used his resulting fortune to develop the Longwood property from 1906 until his death in 1954. His foresight ensured that his beloved Gardens would continue. His vision for the future was built on a few sound principles, allowing those who followed to have the freedom to adapt to changing conditions without distorting the founder's strong sense of excellence, education, and public enjoyment.

Heritage, horticulture, and design are the "soul" of Longwood Gardens. Pierre du Pont and the Peirces before him began a rich tradition of horticulture. Mr. du Pont developed the property for the specific purpose of display, a partnership between design and horticulture. Subsequently, Longwood has evolved as a not-for-profit organization. The highest standards of ethics, safety, leadership, staff development, information exchange, and fiscal responsibility are the "mind" of Longwood; they act as guides to steward Mr. du Pont's legacy of excellence. The Gardens' many audiences (more than 53 million visitors since 1906) and their experiences—garden pleasure, learning, performing arts enjoyment—are the "voice" of Longwood, interpreting and sharing its central character with the world. The physical plant, roads, and environmental stewardship are the "body" of Longwood, the behind-the-scenes architectural and ecological infrastructure that demands unrelenting attention. Finally, Longwood's "public face" is revealed in its interactions with and within the many communities it serves.

A few key principles embody this institution. First is **Preservation**. Pierre du Pont bought the land near Kennett Square in Chester County, Pennsylvania, on July 20, 1906, to save its collection of old trees from a sawmill. He noted that "the property was being denuded for the benefit of the owner before the maturity of the debts incurred for its purchase." Pierre was passionately fond of trees and in 1908 sought a man to prune "who will work absolutely under my direction, removing no branch, dead or alive, unless I specify it to be done." In 1932, he proposed that historic trees become semi-public property, that they be registered, and that even the owners be restricted from cutting, trimming, or injuring them. Today, Longwood goes to great lengths to preserve and replant not only the trees but also the entire 1,083 acres of gardens, woodlands, meadows, and wetlands. Equally important is the preservation of Longwood's buildings, greenhouses, fountains, pipe organ, books, photographs, and archives as well as the intangible spirit that makes Longwood unique.

Second is **Horticulture**. Mr. du Pont desired to grow ordinary plants

OPPOSITE: Nectarine blooms in greenhouse now occupied by the Silver Garden, c. 1947

extraordinarily well, and Longwood has ravishing displays of the best chosen for aesthetic rather than botanical interest. There are 11,122 different types of plants growing indoors and out, representing more than 200 plant families. In addition to old favorites, less well known plants are obtained through plant exploration, collaborations, seed exchanges, and purchases. Longwood conducts trials to select the best ornamentals and, if necessary, breeds new ones. Breeding has focused on such colorful plants as New Guinea impatiens, cannas, and cinerarias. Outstanding cultivars are then named and introduced to the trade. Figuring out how to grow unusual plants in great numbers to bloom at the desired time has resulted in dramatic displays of *Echium wildprettii*, *Geranium maderense*, *Lachenalia* species, *Meconopsis*, and many others. Virus and soil testing, tissue culture, garden mapping, and tracking and labeling nearly 70,000 plants over the past 55 years have also enhanced Longwood's displays. Thousands of plants have been distributed to gardens and institutions around the world. Support of plant exploration has resulted in some 14,734 plant collections from 65 expeditions to 54 countries over the past 62 years, an accomplishment unprecedented in American horticulture.

Next come **Education and Training**, perhaps Longwood's farthest-reaching legacy. Mr. du Pont directed that a school of horticulture be established here, and it came into being starting with international students in 1956, a summer laboratory for college students in 1958, a graduate program in 1967, the Professional Gardener Training Program in 1970, college internships in 1982, high school internships in 1995, and a high school groundskeeping program in 1996. Over the past 62 years, more than 2,000 students have participated, and many have gone on to careers in horticulture. Former students have become presidents or garden managers of the American Horticultural Society, Arnold Arboretum, Birmingham Botanical Gardens, Bloedel Reserve, Brooklyn Botanic Garden, Brookside Gardens, Callaway Gardens, Chanticleer, Chicago Botanic Garden, Dallas Arboretum, Hillwood, Morris Arboretum of the University of Pennsylvania, New England Wild Flower Society, Norfolk Botanical Garden, Opryland Resort, Pennsylvania Horticultural Society, Powell Gardens, Scott Arboretum of Swarthmore College, Smithsonian Institution, United States Botanic Garden, Walt Disney World, Winterthur, and, not surprisingly, Longwood itself. Thousands more professional and amateur gardeners have participated in the 62-year-old Continuing Education Program, and millions of visitors have benefited from on-site labels, signs, hand-outs, programs, and interaction with staff.

Longwood was conceived with and strives to incorporate **Innovation**. Pierre du Pont embraced technology and filled his gardens with it. The Conservatory is classic yet industrial, with tunnels hiding the utilities and a massive heating system. The fountains recall the grandeur of baroque Europe yet also the power of electric pumps to propel water and electric lights to illuminate it. Computers now control not only the fountains but also assist with everything else, including the design of new gardens. Greenhouses feature state-of-the-art technology to optimize growing conditions. Longwood is one of the first places to use LEDs by the thousands for holiday lighting. Even the bugs can't escape innovation. Longwood's Integrated Pest Management program has emerged as a pioneer in its field. Since 1984 the Gardens has drastically reduced its reliance on toxic chemicals, increased the use of biological and cultural control methods, and achieved solutions that permit world-class aesthetics balanced with a safe environment.

Hospitality has been offered to visitors for 200 years, beginning with the 19th-century Peirce family who planted the trees and hosted community picnics and boating parties on the property. Mr. du Pont welcomed visitors who were curious about the old trees, but it wasn't until the Conservatory opened in 1921 that the public came in large numbers. Amenities for today's 1.5 million annual visitors include a Visitor Center, Restaurant, Shop, drinking fountains, benches, electric mobility carts, guided tours, and, most recently, outdoor refreshments. As former director Everitt Miller often said, "The Queen is coming today"*—and Longwood is ready with both creature comforts and unsurpassed beauty.

The **Performing Arts** add a dimension that has no equal in any American garden. For 45 years Pierre du Pont presented large-scale entertainments both indoors and out, a tradition that continues today. Over the past century about 13,000 performances have graced the Gardens, from Open Air Theatre musicales and thunderous organ recitals to Big Band, ballet, and bells. In a larger sense, Longwood exemplifies Pierre's concept of The Garden as Theatre. The flowers, fountains, architecture, and fireworks "wow" the visitors, just as Pierre had been wowed by the theatrical gardens of Italy and France and by the dazzling nineteenth-century World's Fairs he so enjoyed.

Philanthropy is perhaps the least well known of Pierre du Pont's commitments. Although one of the wealthiest men of his generation, his quiet lifestyle and aversion to publicity meant that many of his generous gifts were simply recorded as "anonymous." His sense of community can be traced to his forefathers' strong belief that with resources comes a responsibility to give back to those people and institutions whose work depends on private philanthropy rather than on government support. This family tradition handed down from his great-great-grandfather and namesake Pierre Samuel du Pont de Nemours inspired Pierre to share his fortune with others. During his lifetime, he donated more than $8 million to build more than 120 public schools in Delaware and Pennsylvania. At a time when segregation still smudged society, he financed an entire network of facilities for African American students. The University of

Delaware and his alma mater, M.I.T., also benefited greatly from his generosity. He personally contributed more than $3 million to area hospitals and embarked on a public road improvement program that lasted 48 years and cost several million dollars. Since 1937, his Longwood Foundation has contributed $975 million to support Longwood Gardens and an additional $705 million to support arts and humanities, civic, educational, environmental, health and hospital, housing, and social service organizations in Delaware and southeastern Pennsylvania. This totals more than $3.5 billion in today's dollars.

The Gardens' outreach has been local, regional, national, and international. Gifts from Mr. du Pont, the Foundation, and the Gardens beginning in the 1920s established and have supported the Longwood Fire Company. Today this 143-member volunteer/career organization safeguards residents in surrounding townships and assists neighboring fire companies. Many of the volunteer firefighters have been Longwood employees. The Gardens staff advises community organizations on such matters as street trees and beautification, works with school and service groups, judges flower shows, lectures off site, and shares knowledge with professional organizations and other gardens around the world.

Although the spark of creativity and the means to fulfill its promise came from one man, Longwood has always been an amalgam of devotion and hard work by hundreds, if not thousands, of dedicated individuals—trustees, advisors, employees, students, and volunteers. It would take a separate book to list them all. But the results of their efforts are clearly visible, and they can take justifiable pride in celebrating Longwood's more than a century of garden splendor.

*This quote originated with Bo Callaway of Callaway Gardens, who told it to Longwood Trustee William H. Frederick, Jr., who shared it with Everitt Miller.

1700-1906

The Rise & Fall of Peirce's Park

Longwood's unique story begins more than 200 years before Pierre du Pont arrived on the scene. For generations the region had been inhabited by Native Americans who called themselves the Lenni Lenape, which means the True or Original People. Living off the rich diversity of streams and woods, they fished and foraged for most of their food. At times they constructed dams to maximize the fish harvest. They supplemented their diet by raising maize (corn) and by hunting venison, bear, and elk. Quartz spear points dating back to 2000 BC have been found on and around the property.

In 1700, George Peirce, a Quaker farmer who had emigrated to Philadelphia in 1684 from Bristol, England, purchased 402 acres of this English-claimed land from William Penn's commissioners for 44 pounds sterling. Half the acreage was presented to his daughter on her marriage in 1703. On the remaining land his son Joshua established a homestead in 1709, building a log cabin and clearing the land for a working farm. In 1730, Joshua built the brick farmhouse that, enlarged, still stands today.

In 1798, in keeping with the Quaker attitude toward the study of natural history as a way of understanding the Almighty, Joshua's twin

LEFT: Peirce's Park, 1999

32-year-old grandsons Joshua and Samuel began planting an arboretum that eventually covered 15 acres and ran in densely planted avenues east and south of the house. It was known within 50 years as one of the finest collections of trees in the nation.

The most conspicuous feature of the Peirce arboretum was its conifer collection laid out in parallel allées so closely planted that many trees later succumbed to the crowded conditions. There was also an excellent representation of deciduous trees from Europe, Asia, and North America. Native species such as tulip trees were collected from the wild. Samuel dug small trees and shrubs locally; Joshua traveled by horseback as far north as the Catskill Mountains of New York and south to Maryland's cypress swamps, returning with plants in his saddlebags. Kentucky coffee trees and cucumber magnolias, both natives of western Pennsylvania, were probably collected on these expeditions. Other trees, such as ginkgo and yellow cucumber magnolias, were acquired through plant exchanges with fellow horticulturists and nurserymen.

Samuel died in 1838 and Joshua in 1851, and the farm was inherited by Joshua's son George Washington Peirce. He carefully maintained the plantings, periodically replacing some of the original trees and constantly adding to the collection. He continued to operate the property as a working farm but developed the arboretum into a pleasure ground, in keeping with the parks movement then sweeping America. Croquet courts, rustic summerhouses, and rowboats were added for the enjoyment of guests.

CLOCKWISE FROM TOP LEFT: Joshua Peirce, daguerreotype of a c. 1830-40 painting; George Washington Peirce, c. 1862; Peirce's Park, 1884. OPPOSITE: Peirce family outside Peirce House, 1884.

Parties and picnics at Peirce's Park were frequent neighborhood social occasions. When George Peirce died in 1880, the Park was in its prime, both as an arboretum and as a pleasure garden.

George's heirs showed little interest in horticulture and allowed the Park to deteriorate badly. Finally, in 1905, after more than 200 years of ownership, the Peirce family sold the farm. It was resold twice in the next 14 months. The third buyer immediately made arrangements for the trees to be cut. It was the presence of a sawmill on the property that prompted 36-year-old Pierre du Pont to purchase the farm in 1906, giving birth to Longwood Gardens.

FROM LEFT: Large Lake in Peirce's Park, c. 1884; Boating party on Large Lake at Peirce's Park, c. 1880. OPPOSITE: Ginkgo, yellow cucumber magnolia (the largest in the US), and cucumber magnolia, all planted c. 1800 south of the Peirce-du Pont House, 1975

1870-1954
Pierre S. du Pont

Pierre du Pont's decision to save the trees of Peirce's Park reflects an acute awareness of plants and gardens dating from childhood. The du Pont clan had a long tradition of gardening, and Pierre became one of the family's greatest gardeners.

Pierre was born in 1870 in a DuPont Company house overlooking the Brandywine Creek a few miles north of Wilmington, Delaware. His early years were influenced by the area's natural beauty and by the du Pont family traditions of gardening.

The death of his father Lammot in a chemical explosion at a Company plant in 1884 had far-reaching consequences. Fourteen-year-old Pierre became father to his nine brothers and sisters, providing invaluable training for later accomplishments.

In 1886, he entered the Massachusetts Institute of Technology near Boston. Following graduation in 1890, he secured employment with the DuPont Company in Wilmington. In 1899, Pierre moved to Ohio and

OPPOSITE: Pierre S. du Pont, 1914. FROM TOP: Pierre du Pont, age 5, 1875; 16-year-old Pierre (far right) with his mother and siblings, 1886; St. Amour, 1891. Pierre du Pont laid out the garden here at his family home in 1891. In 1904, he hired professional landscapers to make improvements. His dissatisfaction prompted him to do all his own garden designs thereafter.

became president of the Johnson Company, where he was involved in land development. In 1902, he moved back to Wilmington to again work for the DuPont Company, which had been founded exactly 100 years earlier by his great-grandfather Eleuthère Irénée du Pont (1771-1834) to manufacture gunpowder. Pierre assumed leadership of the Company in various capacities from 1902 to 1954 and guided its transition from a family enterprise to a modern corporation. Under his leadership, DuPont became one of the largest chemical companies in the world by diversifying its

ABOVE: Chemistry class, Massachusetts Institute of Technology. In 1890, Pierre du Pont (third from left) graduated from the Massachusetts Institute of Technology with a degree in chemistry. RIGHT: DuPont Company ad, c. 1930. Due to Pierre du Pont's foresight, DuPont diversified its product line from blasting powder and gunpowder to a wide variety of household and industrial products.

product line from explosives to a wide variety of household and industrial products. Mr. du Pont also directed the development of General Motors from 1915 to 1929. Because of his innovations in transforming these businesses, he is often regarded as the father of the modern corporation.

With business success came great wealth and a responsibility to use it wisely. "I wonder why so many people hang on to their fortune and property instead of having fun watching the distribution processes themselves," he declared in 1922. Pierre du Pont was one of the Delaware Valley's leading philanthropists. He and his wife Alice gave in excess of $8 million to

LEFT: DuPont Company ad, 1951. ABOVE: In the 1920s, Pierre du Pont formed a fire brigade to protect the Gardens. By 1926, it was named the Longwood Fire Company, and it has served the entire community ever since. This truck was purchased by Mr. du Pont in the 1920s.

build more than 120 public schools in Delaware and Pennsylvania, and he donated $2 million to the University of Delaware. He contributed more than $3 million to area hospitals, providing over $1 million to the Chester County Hospital alone. He also embarked on a public road improvement program which lasted 48 years and cost several million dollars. Since 1937, more than $1.6 billion [$3.5 billion in today's dollars] have been distributed through foundations he created.

Pierre always preferred to reside amid the quiet, familiar beauty of the Brandywine Valley rather than relocate to a large metropolis. But he liked to travel, which introduced all sorts of influences. There was no better place to see the latest technology than at the monumental world's fairs of the late nineteenth century. As a six-year-old, Pierre was mesmerized by a huge display of water pumps in action at Philadelphia's 1876 Centennial Exposi-

tion. At 19, he enjoyed the Exposition Universelle in Paris with its new Eiffel Tower. Pierre was 23 when the World Columbian Exposition in Chicago astounded him with grandiose architecture and illuminated fountains. As his personal resources and professional experience grew and he started building for himself, he logically drew upon these technical innovations and architectural styles.

FROM LEFT: Pierre du Pont and Alice Belin du Pont on their honeymoon, 1915; Alice and Pierre du Pont laying the cornerstone for an addition to the Chester County Hospital, 1924; Alice du Pont (left) receiving a silver basket filled with flowers that reads: "In Loving Appreciation Alice Belin du Pont from the women of Chester County, Penna. September 8, 1923."
OPPOSITE: Pierre S. du Pont High School, Wilmington, DE, c. 1935. This is the only school that bears Pierre du Pont's name because he opposed such honors.

Travel also introduced him to a wide variety of garden settings, including Horticultural Hall at the 1876 Centennial, England's Sydenham Crystal Palace, the garden maze at Hampton Court, and the Royal Botanic Gardens at Kew, as well as to the flora of South America, the Caribbean, Florida, California, and Hawaii. Visits to more than 20 Italian villas and 50 French châteaux focused on the architectural qualities and water effects of those gardens. His extensive collection of garden books, especially the lavish folios that documented European landscapes, reinforced the impressions made on these trips.

Pierre's own building and gardening experiences prior to acquiring Longwood included overseeing construction of the new family homestead when he was only 21; owning a commercial florist business with seven greenhouses at age 28; and supervising the building of 150 houses with rudimentary landscaping at age 29. At 34, he hired professional landscapers to improve the family estate but was so disappointed with an initial site survey that he did his own designs from then on. At 35, he headed up the team that built the 12-story DuPont Building in Wilmington, Delaware. When at 36 years of age he purchased Peirce's Park, he was well qualified to begin its transformation into Longwood Gardens, even if he didn't yet know that he was going to do it.

LEFT: Fountain at Pierre's childhood home Nemours, c. 1882. OPPOSITE, CLOCKWISE FROM TOP LEFT: Evening fountain display at World Columbian Exposition, 1893; 4-arched private conservatory in Philadelphia, 1880, where Pierre decided that if he built a greenhouse it would be open to the public; Visiting Italian gardens, 1913; Pump display at Philadelphia Centennial, 1876.

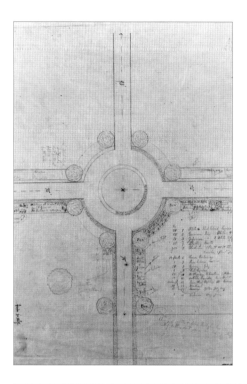

1906-1916

A Country Place

In July 1906, Pierre du Pont purchased all rights to historic Peirce's Park and surrounding lands, totaling over 202 acres (today enlarged to 1,083), for approximately $16,000. He had no intention of using the place as a primary residence, and he wasn't planning to build lavish gardens. "I have recently experienced what I would formerly have diagnosed as an attack of insanity; that is, I have purchased a small farm about ten miles from [Wilmington]," he wrote to a friend. However, "I expect to have a good deal of enjoyment in restoring its former condition and making it a place where I can entertain my friends." Pierre later recalled that the real reason for acquiring the farm was to save the collection of old trees.

He soon was calling the place Longwood after the Longwood Meeting House, which in turn was named for a neighboring Longwood Farm on part of the original Peirce land. "Longwood" probably derives from a nearby stretch of forest known as The Long Woods.

In 1907, Pierre laid out Longwood's first true flower garden. He filled the 600-foot-long Flower Garden Walk with favorite perennials and biennials, and with some annuals. A pool about 20 feet in diameter was

OPPOSITE: Flower Garden Walk, c. 1913-1916. TOP RIGHT: Garden plan drawn by Pierre du Pont, 1907. RIGHT: Flower Garden Walk with cornfield beyond, 1909

constructed at the intersection of the main paths. Its simple jet of water was Longwood's first fountain.

Although his later gardens would draw heavily on Italian and French forms, this early garden reflected what he termed an "old-fashioned" influence, with nostalgic cottage-garden flowers, exuberant shrubs, rose-laden trellises, picturesque benches, a Peacock Arbor, birdbath, and even a shiny "gazing ball." The scale was grand, the accessories quaint. From this first axial layout Longwood Gardens has grown, albeit in piecemeal fashion as the mood touched its creator.

The springtime effect of the new Flower Garden was so successful that in 1909 Mr. du Pont hosted a garden party in June. Four hundred people attended and dined on typical garden party fare costing him $1.50 per person. A local infantry band was the musical entertainment, and fireworks provided a fitting climax to a lovely evening. Garden parties were held most years from 1909 until 1916 and from 1919 until 1931, with one last affair in 1940 (which now cost him $3.85 per person for 1,200 guests). These fetes became the highlight of the summer social season and no doubt encouraged Pierre to look for ever more wonderful ways to delight his guests.

In 1910 and 1913, Pierre and his future wife, Alice Belin, visited

LEFT, CLOCKWISE FROM TOP: Flower Garden fountain, before 1920; Glazing Ball, c. 1922; Rose Garden, 1922 (now Wisteria Garden). OPPOSITE: Sundial Garden, c. 1913-1916 (now Peony Garden).

Italy. At the Villa d'Este outside Rome, famous for its fountains, he reportedly remarked, "It would be nice to have something like this at home." On the second trip they visited at least 23 villas and gardens, including the Villa Gori in Siena whose outdoor theatre provided the inspiration for one at Longwood. On his return, Pierre had the site of the original Peirce barn excavated, brought in stone to form retaining walls around a 68-foot-wide stage, and planted the wings on either side with hemlock (now arborvitae).

The debut of the theatre at a garden party in June 1914 was a huge success. A local paper reported that just after dark, electric lights were turned on to illuminate the stage for a series of period dances. The finale was a "frolic by the harlequins, who, much to the surprise of the guests, danced among them, throwing confetti and garden roses, then winding their way out in a path of light, finally disappearing amid the trees." Two weeks after this tremendously successful party, Pierre began experimenting with water jets installed in the theatre stage, which first gushed at the 1915 garden party. These "secret" fountains drenched visiting nieces and nephews, to their delight.

Longwood in the early years was enchanting during warm weather but, Pierre noted, "rather dreary in winter" with visitors "few and far between." Perhaps this is why in 1914 he built an L-shaped extension onto the original Peirce farmhouse, doubling its size. The house had its

OPPOSITE: Florence Noyes Dancers at the 1915 Garden Party. FROM TOP: Louisa Copeland, Pierre du Pont, Alice Belin on the outdoor stage, Villa Gori, Siena, Italy, 1913; Longwood's Open Air Theatre, 1915 Garden Party; First "secret" fountains on the Theatre stage, c. 1915.

share of country place amenities: a bowling alley, automatic fire doors, counterweighted windows that lowered into the basement, and a built-in rug-rolling machine. Connecting the old and new wings was a conservatory, Longwood's first "winter garden" and Pierre's first experience with the aesthetics of greenhouse gardening. Its courtyard is luxuriously planted with exotic foliage and is graced with a small marble fountain, a wedding present to mark Pierre's marriage in 1915 to Alice Belin, his favorite traveling companion. Longwood now had a First Lady.

ABOVE: Architect's rendering of addition to the Peirce-du Pont House, c. 1913. RIGHT: Pierre and Alice du Pont in Garden Party attire, c. 1916. OPPOSITE: Peirce-du Pont House conservatory, 1928.

1916-1926

Grand-Style Gardening

Pierre du Pont's earliest Longwood greenhouse was 132' long by 25' wide, built in 1912 to grow flowers, vegetables, and grapes. His 1914 house addition was a true conservatory, designed as an enclosed garden living room. He must have been pleased because by 1916 he was contemplating much grander facilities "designed to exploit the sentiments and ideas associated with plants and flowers in a large way." The practicality of his vision was no doubt bolstered by his experience as president of the DuPont Engineering Company that had handled $130 million of World War I construction. After the war, a new Conservatory was planned by architect Alexander J. Harper, but the design was completed by J. Walter Cope and the DuPont Engineering Company, with Pierre critiquing every detail. Longwood's largest construction project officially opened on November 25, 1921.

OPPOSITE: Exhibition Hall, 2010. CLOCKWISE FROM TOP LEFT: Building Conservatory, 1920; Constructing Exhibition Hall, 1919-1920; Orangery with mums and citrus, 1921.

The overall effect suggests a European *orangerie* (used to overwinter tender fruit trees in cold climates) with a symmetrical façade and arched bronze windows set in aggregate-covered concrete. The central building is 181 feet wide by 204 feet deep, shaped into a "T" with a 25-foot-tall colonnade around the interior edge; the ridge of the central roof rises about 40 feet. While the walls and windows suggest pre-Industrial classicism, the roof is akin to the great 19th-century exhibition halls, permitting maximum light penetration. On either side of the main building are long, low houses (not unlike pergolas) connected to end pavilions. The latest technology was used to heat, water, and power the complex, but the systems are hidden in tunnels so as not to detract from the grandeur of the glass-covered peristyle and surrounding rooms.

Pierre du Pont chose to fill his new garden not with the usual jungle

LEFT: Chrysanthemums in Orangery, 2003. BELOW: Boilers, 1926. OPPOSITE, CLOCKWISE FROM TOP: Conservatory exterior; Orangery, 1921; Exhibition Hall, 1922, before construction of Music Room at far end.

of exotic tropical foliage in botanical fashion but with fruits and flowers used in a decorative, horticultural way. One 1921 observer termed the greenhouses "floral sun parlors." The center hall (Orangery) was filled with citrus surrounded by cypress trees, acacias, tree ferns, banana, coffee, guava, kumquats, mango, papaya, begonias, fuchsia, heliotrope, lantana, orchids, plumbago, and African violets. Azaleas bloomed in spring, chrysanthemums in autumn and at Christmas. Eventually the citrus was phased out because of poor fruit production, and flowering plants surrounding manicured lawns became the floral focal point, a design approach used to this day.

A late winter display in the 1920s might have included pink amaryllis, white calla lilies, blue cineraria, pink cyclamen, Easter lilies, geranium standards, and wisteria. Next to the walkways glowed lavender and white crocuses, yellow daffodils, forget-me-nots, pink, lavender, cream and white hyacinths, lily-of-the-valley, pink tulips, and violets. Blooming roses climbed the concrete pillars while fruit trees were laden with pink blossoms. Oranges and grapefruit were in fruit and bananas were in bud. Roses, carnations, gardenias, hibiscus, tuberous begonias, sweet peas, snapdragons, primroses, and freesias blanketed the production greenhouses with scented bloom. Dazzling collections of acacias, amaryllis, azaleas, camellias, and orchids flourished in the protected climate.

Indoor fruit and vegetable production was an important part of the

LEFT: Orangery, c. 1992. OPPOSITE: Eastern Guernsey Breeder's Association luncheon in Exhibition Hall, 1925.

horticultural operation during Mr. du Pont's lifetime. Apricots, nectarines and peaches thrived in the long wings on both sides of the Orangery, plus bananas in the westernmost house. Houses were devoted to figs, grapes, melons, and pineapples. Experimental plantings of coffee, coconut palm, custard apples, feijoa, loquats, persimmons, pomegranates, tea shrubs, and vanilla vines were tried. Cauliflower, celery, butterhead lettuce, and tomatoes were raised indoors, along with flowers for cut arrangements.

A staff of 8 gardeners (in 1922) oversaw this perpetual indoor flower show, aided by 3 boiler operators. Outdoors there were 11 gardeners and groundskeepers, and the entire Horticulture Department of 29 was headed by old-school English gardener William Mulliss.

It would be hard to imagine a more theatrical setting for the display

OPPOSITE, CLOCKWISE FROM TOP LEFT: Tomatoes, 1920s; Melon House, 1922; Pineapples, 1921; Nectarines, 1960s; Greenhouse grapes. RIGHT: Gardeners in Potting Shed, c. 1948.

of plants, unless it would be to the music of a massive 3,650-pipe Aeolian organ added in 1921 on which many of the leading organists of the day performed for both invited guests and for the public. In 1923 an elegant Music Room designed by J. Walter Cope was built opening onto the central axis of the main greenhouse, with walnut paneling, damask-covered walls, teak floors, and a molded plaster ceiling in the most refined drawing room tradition.

The public came in droves, fulfilling Pierre's childhood dream of building a greenhouse open to the public. Mr. and Mrs. du Pont also had the perfect place for grand entertainments, and they hosted innumerable civic and educational groups as well as family and friends. The guests' reactions were always the same: a place beyond compare.

By the mid 1920s, Longwood's indoor facilities were astounding, unlike any in the country. But there was much more to build, both indoors and out.

LEFT: Exhibition Hall set for entertaining, 1922. The organ console protrudes from the far columns. ABOVE: Organist Wilmer Highfield (1882-1947) at the first Aeolian console in the Exhibition Hall, c. 1922. OPPOSITE, CLOCKWISE FROM TOP: Music Room, 1928; Music Room ceiling corner after restoration, 2005; Music Room ceiling ornament, 2005.

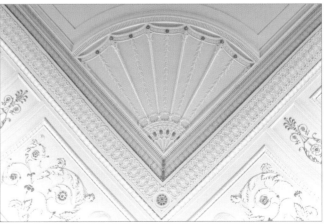

1926-1936
Flowers, Fountains & Music

For several years following the opening of the Conservatory, Pierre and Alice du Pont hosted public and private musical events in the Exhibition Hall. In the winter, however, it became increasingly difficult to stage indoor events with floor seating because of floral displays in the sunken area.

In 1926, Pierre asked Wilmington, DE, architect E. William Martin to design a greenhouse theatre extending eastward from the Exhibition Hall and twice as large. But Pierre abandoned this idea, and plans were finalized for a large greenhouse on the same site designed primarily for non-hardy azaleas and camellias. The building was finished in 1928.

The Azalea House resembled a grand 19th-century exposition shed with 2 rows of structural columns and 3 sections of ridge-and-furrow roof. The sunken center was planted with a magnificent collection of azaleas and rhododendrons painstakingly imported from Belgium, England, and the Arnold Arboretum in Massachusetts. Beyond an imposing fountain was an equally impressive collection of camellias. The house was a riot of color in late winter and early spring.

OPPOSITE: Main Fountain Garden, 2004. FROM TOP: Camellias, 1957; Azalea House, 1963.

Pierre then decided to build an adjoining concert hall to house a new pipe organ and again chose E. William Martin as architect. The 103'-long by 35'-wide Ballroom features damask-covered walls, an elaborate walnut parquet floor, two massive brass and crystal chandeliers, and 14 wall sconces. The ceiling is made of 1,104 panes of rose-colored etched glass originally lit from above by daylight that came through a clear glass roof.

The new Aeolian organ was twice as large as the earlier organ (which Pierre gave to the University of Delaware) and was designed by his private organist, Firmin Swinnen. It has 10,010 pipes ranging in size from 3/4" to 32' long. Real chimes, drums, cymbal, tambourine, xylophone, castanets, and 9-foot concert grand piano are playable from the organ console, and a roll player could play the entire organ automatically. The instrument weighs 55 tons and is installed in 9 chambers that, together, are 63 feet

FROM LEFT: Ballroom, 1999; Firmin Swinnen at the Aeolian console, 1934; Longwood Organ at the Aeolian factory, 1929. OPPOSITE: Longwood's 32'-long pedal pipes at the Aeolian factory in Garwood NJ, 1929.

wide, 23 feet deep, and 40 feet tall. The organ cost $122,700 and was officially inaugurated in June 1930. It is one of the world's largest residence organs and superbly suited for transcriptions of Mr. du Pont's favorite symphonic music.

With the Azalea House and Ballroom, Pierre's vision for indoor facilities was complete. Now he turned his full attention outdoors, where Longwood's hydraulic splendors were already underway.

Pierre and Alice du Pont's summer of 1925 had been capped by a trip to France and a memorable two-week tour of 50 châteaux and gardens, including a visit to Monet's garden hosted by the painter himself. Back home, Pierre constructed from 1925 to 1927 an "Italian" Water Garden in a low-lying, marshy site northeast of Longwood's Large Lake. He chose for inspiration not a recently visited French garden, but the Villa Gamberaia, near Florence, Italy, which he had enjoyed in 1913. He probably based his plan on one published in a garden book. He took into account visual foreshortening by making the farther pair of rectangular pools 14 feet longer than the nearer pair; this ensures that all 4 pools appear proportionately equal when viewed from the elevated observation terrace.

The Italian original has only a few fountains, but in Longwood's Water Garden more than 600 jets in 9 separate displays shoot from 6 blue-tiled pools and from 12 pedestal basins along the sides. Pierre filled

FROM TOP: Villa Gamberaia near Florence, Italy, c. 1920; Longwood's Italian Water Garden under construction, 1926; Italian Water Garden, 1930s. OPPOSITE: Italian Water Garden, c. 1930.

about 50 pages with handwritten calculations to figure out the hydraulic requirements. At maximum capacity 4,500 gallons per minute are recirculated, with the tallest jet in the far pool 40 feet high. A surprise feature is a curving water staircase to the southwest which complements a traditional staircase to the southeast. The arched wall that connects them and supports the observation terrace is embellished with sculptured fountains and terra cotta jars.

The garden was planted with lindens along both sides and with evergreens at the far end; English ivy borders the pools. Limestone copings, pedestal basins, and ornaments carved in Philadelphia and Italy add a distinctively Italian flavor. Yet in its setting within a wooded clearing and in concentration of jets, the garden resembles more a fanciful water bosquet at Versailles. Its full beauty is revealed only by walking down into the garden to see the backlit water shimmering against the deep green foliage.

At the same time, Pierre installed a Sylvan Fountain at the end of the central allée in Peirce's Park. The main jet is 40 feet tall and is a restful eye-catcher when viewed from the house. It is said that Mrs. du Pont could turn it on for her house guests with a push button. The water disappears underground then reappears at the south end of the Italian Water Garden as it noisily cascades down a small waterfall then into two rustic pools on its way back to the pumphouse. When elevation changes permitted, Pierre took advantage of gravity as much as possible!

OPPOSITE: Italian Water Garden, 2003. CLOCKWISE FROM UPPER RIGHT: Sylvan Fountain in Peirce's Park, 1992; Water returning from Sylvan Fountain, 1998; Side pedestal fountains, 1998.

Pierre next decided to enlarge the Open Air Theatre. It had been used since 1914 for theatrical performances, garden parties, concerts, and as a place of amusement for Mr. du Pont's nieces and nephews. The grassy seating area was flat, which restricted visibility, so in 1926 the area under the stage was excavated and spacious underground dressing rooms were built. The soil that was removed was used to give the proper slope to the auditorium.

Longwood's Theatre has since hosted hundreds of performing arts events, reflecting Pierre du Pont's passion for the performing arts. Philadelphia's Savoy Company, the world's oldest amateur theater troupe dedicated to Gilbert and Sullivan, has performed in it most years since 1916. Wilmington's Brandywiners arrived in 1932 and have presented an annual Broadway-style musical ever since. Other entertainments featured famous dancers like Ruth St. Denis, Ted Shawn, Martha Graham, and Doris Humphrey; American Legion pageants; massed choruses; Shakespeare; John Philip Sousa and his Band; and the United States Marine Band. Today, events reflecting all types of performing arts are presented continuously throughout the summer. When the weather cooperates, there is no more beautiful setting.

OPPOSITE, CLOCKWISE FROM TOP LEFT: Brandywiners' *Princess Ida*, 1935; Savoy Company's *Mikado*, 2003; Pierre du Pont with John Philip Sousa, 1930; Pierre du Pont with the United States Marine Band in the Open Air Theatre, 1927. RIGHT, FROM TOP: Brandywine Ballet, 1997; United States Marine Band, 1986.

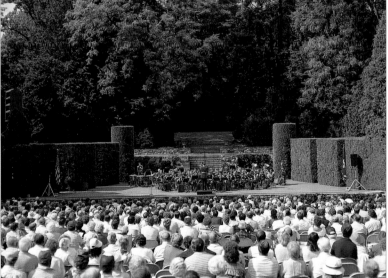

A much enlarged fountain system was installed during the 1926-27 Theatre expansion, with 7 circular basins with removable covers built into the main stage floor, a unique 10'-high water curtain, 2 upper level basins, and isolated roof fountains off to either side. Beneath the stage are 11 pumps recirculating 2,000 gallons of water per minute through 750 nozzles illuminated from below by over 600 lights in red, blue, green, white, and—added in 1933—yellow. The jets and lights were originally controlled from a hand-operated switchboard in the spotlight tower behind the audience.

Nothing like this had ever before been seen! Describing a 1928 public showing, the newspapers noted that the new fountains were "like fireworks, rockets upside down, or weird deep-sea mysteries of coral and fan-shaped fungus, colored in turn ghostly violet or flaming gold, fiery scarlet, yellow, blue and green." Even today they are unique. The color is intense, and the introduction of compressed air into the jets at the end of a display produces a thrilling and unexpected finale as the fountains are rocketed 50 feet up into the trees.

FROM TOP: Enlarging Open Air Theatre, 1927; Constructing stage fountain basins, 1927; Fountain control board, 1958. OPPOSITE: Open Air Theatre fountains at night.

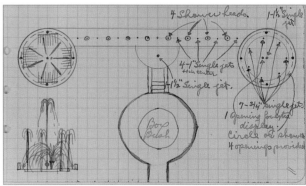

Mr. du Pont was inspired by the success of the Italian Water Garden and the Theatre to create the ultimate fountain display to rival that which he had enjoyed at the 1893 World Columbian Exposition in Chicago 35 years earlier. The area directly south of the Conservatory had been planted in 1921 with boxwood and a U-shaped allée of Norway maples. To this he added, beginning in 1928, two long canals and two circular pools in the area bounded by the maples, and a huge rectangular basin on the far hill.

OPPOSITE, TOP: Initial planting of Main Fountain Garden, 1921. ABOVE: Same view, 1939.

OPPOSITE, FROM LOWER LEFT: Maple Allée, 1928; R. P. Brewer's original sketch for the Lower Canal, 1929.

The pools and basins were filled with 380 fountainheads, and a recirculation system of 18 pumps propelled as much as 10,000 gallons of water a minute as high as 130 feet. Adjoining reservoirs supplied a 50-foot mini-Niagara cascading next to a French-inspired Chimes Tower. The entire system held 675,000 gallons of water.

TOP: SE corner of the Main Fountain Garden, 1930s. LEFT: Chimes Tower and Waterfall, 1934. OPPOSITE: Lower Canal at night, 1950s.

The Main Fountains were first turned on in 1931, but it was not until several years later that the 5-acre garden was finished. Tons of limestone carved into decorative flowers, fruit, and water creatures were shipped from Italy by the Florentine firm Olivotti to impart an Old World feeling. To give a green background, Pierre turned the adjoining cornfield into an instant landscape with several hundred mature trees and shrubs, some as high as 70 feet tall. These were transplanted from estates, nurseries, and from the wild throughout 14 states by Lewis and Valentine, the country's foremost tree movers.

But the stonework and plantings are rendered invisible at night when

TOP, FROM LEFT: Wall fountains and Loggia, c. 1935; Carved limestone lion and sea serpents in Main Fountain Garden, 1975. LEFT: Transplanting mature tree into the Main Fountain Garden, c. 1928. OPPOSITE: Upper Canal inspired by the Villa d'Este, 1950s.

the fountains assume a new dimension. 724 lighting units with colored glass filters tinted the water red, blue, green, yellow, and white, with every conceivable variation in between. The spectacle is managed from a small room beneath the observation terrace in front of the Conservatory. The original control board had more than 200 toggle switches and 100 small levers to activate the pumping and dimming equipment located in the pump house at the opposite end of the garden. This system was replaced in 1965 with a modern theatre lighting board, but it was not until 1984 when the system was computerized and synchronized to music that its true artistic potential could be realized.

From a garden history point of view, the Main Fountain Garden combines Italianate ornamentation and French grandeur with World's Fair showmanship. Like other great fountains, it is an engineering *tour de force* using the latest technology of the time.

The completion of the fountains in the mid 1930s marked an end to major construction during Mr. du Pont's lifetime. He was in his mid 60s and had been able to create something that far exceeded his 1906 goal to make "a place where I could entertain my friends." Besides, what else was there to build? More importantly, the social and political climate was changing. Pierre du Pont had been an astute investor and remained so despite the economic downturn. His main task now was to figure out how to ensure Longwood's future.

OPPOSITE: Rectangular Basin in Main Fountain Garden, 2004. CLOCKWISE FROM TOP LEFT: Main Fountain Garden Pumphouse, 1958; Longwood's fountain control systems were devised by R. P. Brewer, shown here at the Main Fountain control board, 1958; Aerial view of fountains and Conservatory, 1931.

1936-1946
Ensuring Longwood's Future

Pierre and Alice du Pont enjoyed traveling in the 1920s and '30s, visiting Europe 7 times between 1925 and 1937. Most trips included a visit to the Belin family's ancestral Château d'Andelot in eastern France, which Pierre had co-purchased in 1924 with Alice's brother. Nearby was the world's oldest analemmatic sundial at the church of Brou, in Bourg-en-Bresse. Pierre was so intrigued that from 1937 to 1939 he designed and constructed a similar but larger 30 by 36-foot oval analemmatic sundial along with a new Rose Garden on the site of a former vegetable field east of the Main Fountain Garden. Mr. du Pont and staff members spent years taking on-site readings and calibrating the figure 8 markings in the center of the dial upon which a moveable gnomon casts a thin shadow marking the time. The dial was recalibrated periodically until more accurate markings were achieved in the mid 1970s.

Life at Longwood continued uneventfully through the 1930s. The annual Christmas Party hosted by Mr. and Mrs. du Pont was always a highlight for employees and their children, who each received one good toy, clothing, and goodies. For the du Ponts' friends, one last Garden Party was held in 1940. About 1,200 guests were received in the new

FROM TOP: Plotting the Analemmatic Sundial, c. 1940; Pierre and Alice du Pont making final preparations for the annual Employee Christmas Party, mid to late 1920s.

Sundial Garden, and they dined in the greenhouses on the usual party fare. For entertainment, the Montgomery Ballet presented five dances in the Open Air Theatre, including *An American in Paris*.

In addition to horticulture, agriculture had always been important at Longwood, which started out, after all, as a farm. Pierre du Pont was a "gentleman farmer." He sought to create a self-sustaining model farm that used the latest farming techniques and methods. In reality the farm was more an expansive, expensive hobby than a business, but it did produce food for the du Ponts and their employees. Pierre purchased 25 contiguous properties over the years, and Longwood's original 202 acres grew to 926 by 1935. The farms and vegetable garden were staffed by as many as 34 employees. All sorts of vegetables, fruit, and prize-winning livestock were raised, much to the delight of Alice du Pont. A curious highlight was a Guernsey cow, Longwood Jewess, who with great fanfare was exhibited and gave birth in Borden's Dairy World of Tomorrow at the 1939 New York World's Fair. Pierre shared his agricultural experiences with other socially prominent gentlemen farmers as a member of Philadelphia's Farmer's Club from 1929 to 1954.

Longwood's agricultural and horticultural operations slowed considerably during World War II. The 9-hole golf course (where the Parking Lot is now) and tennis courts were eliminated. Many employees served in the Armed Forces, and a 72-bed hospital was set up in rooms adjoining the Ballroom just in case the community needed it. Pierre noted, "We are having very few visitors these days, practically none. The place seems

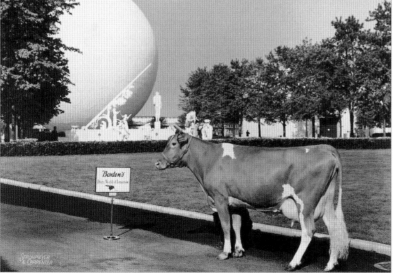

FROM TOP: The Webb Barn built 1919 east of the Italian Water Garden to house the prize-winning dairy herd, c. 1930; Longwood's celebrity cow at the 1939 New York World's Fair.

deserted and less like a public park." Even the brass fountain nozzles were hidden for fear they would be confiscated for metal. Then in 1944 Alice du Pont died after a short illness. Pierre initially retreated to his apartment in Wilmington's Hotel du Pont during weekdays, visiting Longwood only on weekends. But he was more concerned than ever about Longwood's future, particularly since he had no children but considered the Gardens part of the du Pont family legacy.

In 1913 the federal government had enacted personal income tax. In response Pierre incorporated Longwood in 1914. He always tried to stay one step ahead of the IRS to keep his farm and gardens in the best possible tax situation, and in 1937 the Longwood Foundation was created to handle his charitable giving. Finally, in 1946 the government gave approval for the Foundation to operate Longwood as a public garden with tax-exempt status "for the sole use of the public for purposes of exhibition, instruction, education, and enjoyment."

Longwood was safe, and Pierre du Pont could relax just a bit, but he would never be able to truly retire because all kinds of projects, business and otherwise, kept him on the go.

ABOVE: Portrait of Pierre and Alice du Pont at Longwood Gardens by N. de Molas, a Russian painter of stylized estate landscapes, 1936.

1946-1956
Private to Public

After Alice's death, Pierre du Pont directed his energies towards historical research. He collected and translated hundreds of old family documents from French into English, and he compiled a detailed family genealogy dating back to the year 1500. His interest in history evolved into an idea to house the collection in the Peirce-du Pont House and to open it to scholars as The Longwood Library. (In 1961 the collection was moved to the Hagley Library near Wilmington.) He continued perfecting the analemmatic sundial and also devised and copyrighted a perpetual calendar and a moon calendar. The Gardens were maintained as always, augumented by the inheritance of Mrs. William K. du Pont's famous orchid collection. Outdoors, farming operations were discontinued in 1951 except for fruit orchards and a small vegetable garden.

A highlight of these final years was the 150th anniversary of the du Pont family's arrival in the United States, held at Longwood on January 1, 1950, with 632 family members from around the world in attendance. Pierre had long been head of the clan or, as one writer has noted, the "maximum du Pont chieftain...the first among equals in a family of tycoons." How appropriate that they should celebrate at the family's best-known cultural legacy. With characteristic modesty, Pierre noted about

RIGHT: Pierre du Pont at Longwood, 1949.

Longwood, "In these days my part of the work is small, but I am happy to be able to keep the place going."

Pierre's biggest obligation was as star witness in the federal anti-trust suit against DuPont and General Motors held in Chicago. He spent months preparing, and he testified periodically from November 1952 until February 1954, no easy task for someone in their 80s.

In 1954, Mr. du Pont was recognized by the French government for his lifetime of achievement and generosity to the people of France. He was awarded the *Cravate de Commandeur* of the French Legion of Honor at a special dinner at Longwood on April 2. Three days later, on April 5, Pierre du Pont was stricken at Longwood with severe abdominal pain and rushed to the hospital in Wilmington where he died from a ruptured aorta. A fitting memorial service was held in the Peirce-du Pont House conservatory,

filled to overflowing with flowers, family, friends, and employees. Pierre is buried next to Alice in the du Pont family cemetery near Wilmington.

With his usual foresight, Pierre had in place a well-funded yet adaptable mechanism for Longwood to continue. Five very experienced businessmen (his nephews) were already the trustees of the Longwood Foundation, and they soon started searching for a professional director.

Dr. George Beadle, Professor of Biology at the California Institute of Technology, suggested they consider Dr. Russell J. Seibert. Seibert was experienced in plants, farming, horticulture, agriculture, plant economics, government, and public garden administration. He was born on a farm in Belleville, Illinois, in 1914. After a youth spent plowing his father's fields, he vowed "there must be a better way to make a living than looking at a horse's rear end all day." Seibert received a bachelor's degree in geology and a Master of Science and Ph.D. in botany from Washington University, St. Louis, Missouri. He collected plants during the summers of 1935, 1937, and 1938 in Panama for the Missouri Botanical Garden, and he performed rubber plant surveys and established rubber plant stations in Central and South America as an agent for the United States Department of Agriculture (USDA) from 1940 to 1949. After a short stint as a geneticist with the USDA in Beltsville, MD, he became the director of the Los Angeles State and County Arboretum in 1950.

On July 20, 1955, Russell Seibert (1914-2004) began as Longwood's first director. The charge from the Board of Trustees was to "transform a private estate into an internationally recognized horticultural display." Within three months, Seibert had outlined a future for Longwood that continues to this day. As he noted to the Trustees: "In this age of mechanical, chemical, electronic and atomic miracles, we need not fear a decline in the powers of Nature. Rather, a feeling of closeness to Nature through Horticulture and Gardening shall be one of the potent stabilizers of our civilization. The veracity of this statement is fully evidenced by the fact that home gardening is the 'No.1' hobby of the American public today. Through Longwood Gardens and its program of outstanding horticultural display, every visitor to the Gardens has the opportunity to gain, culturally and spiritually, a better peace of mind."

Longwood was in good hands.

OPPOSITE, FROM LEFT: Pierre du Pont receiving the French Legion of Honor from Pierre Donzelot, 1954; Russell J. Seibert, Longwood's first professional director, 1955; Longwood staff, 1955. RIGHT: Visitors and parking west of the Conservatory, c. 1955.

1956–1966
Educating
the Public

The late 1950s and early 1960s saw tremendous change at Longwood, comparable to the building program of the 1920s except the emphasis was now on public comfort and education. Russell Seibert immediately proposed a course of action that has been followed in spirit, if not almost to the letter, to the present.

Three months after assuming the directorship, he proposed funding fellowships and research pertaining to horticultural display, including plant introductions and a cooperative program with the University of Delaware. He suggested a master landscape plan and a horticultural display expert. The indoors needed less espaliered fruit but new and expanded collections of orchids, plant curiosities, foliage plants, bromeliads, insectivorous plants, tropicals, and medicinal plants. And a better visitor route through the Conservatory on crowded days. The outdoors called for more variety of vegetables and herbs, with the best shrubs and small trees for the home garden.

The public's chief complaint was the lack of labels, which were desperately needed in addition to a plant records system. Seibert wanted closer relations with garden clubs and plant societies both locally and

RIGHT: Pruning demonstration for the public at the northwest edge of the future Parking Lot, 1957.

nationally. He envisioned tours, lectures and classes, cooperation with high schools and universities, awards, an information desk, publications for sale, first-class photography, grounds transportation, and a library. He proposed immediate safety and road improvements, increased public parking, more benches, ponds for water conservation and fire protection, and picnic grounds.

A major personnel challenge was to establish consistent employee policies after years of perceived inequality resulting from the idiosyncrasies of Longwood as one man's estate.

In 1956, Everitt Miller was hired to understudy John Marx, Mr. du Pont's chief horticulturist. Miller became the most influential staff player other than Seibert and would eventually succeed him as director. The existing Departments of Horticulture (responsible for the plants and gardens, under Marx), Maintenance (buildings and utilities, under Russell Brewer), and Business (accounting and personnel, under Mr. du Pont's former secretary George Thompson, Sr.) were augmented by a new Department of Education led by Dr. Walter Hodge, whom Seibert met when they both worked in Peru during World War II. Together, the staff initiated Seibert's vision with major improvements to visitor services and education, to the Gardens' public display facilities, and to the science of horticulture as practiced at Longwood.

In 1956, the first Information Center, designed by E. William Martin, opened at the west end of the Conservatory adjoining the original visitor parking area. The Center was small but offered Longwood's first

FROM TOP: First Information Center, 1955 sketch; Guided tour, 1963; School tour, 1963.
OPPOSITE: Dr. Donald Huttleston leading garden club tour, c. 1956.

publications, guide maps and brochures, personnel to answer questions, guided tours, and restrooms.

In the Conservatory, the visitor circulation problem was solved by connecting the stand-alone Rose House to a new Desert House in 1957 and Tropical Terrace in 1958 (both designed by the architectural firm of Victorine and Samuel Homsey, Inc.), allowing a one-way pedestrian traffic loop. Fruit and vegetable houses were turned into display houses, especially with the newly planted Geographic House in 1958. A collection of bonsai was purchased in 1959.

Outdoors, irrigation ponds were constructed beginning in 1957, but the most memorable ponds were the breathtaking Waterlily Display opening that same year. Russell Seibert had seen at firsthand the beauty of tropical aquatics. It didn't hurt that his father-in-law was George Pring, renowned waterlily and orchid expert and former superintendent of the Missouri Botanical Garden. Pring helped design the 13-pool display, along with Russell Brewer who had engineered Longwood's fountains. The Missouri Botanic Garden supplied the plants, and Pring mentored gardener Patrick Nutt, who went on in 1960 to hybridize Longwood's giant waterplatters. Their 7-foot-wide rimmed leaves often grow 3 to 6 inches daily, weigh up to 10 pounds, and can support upwards of 150

OPPOSITE, CLOCKWISE FROM LEFT: Tropical Terrace, 1995; Desert House, 1959; Geographic House, 1962. ABOVE, CLOCKWISE FROM TOP LEFT: George Pring and Patrick Nutt, 1957; Building waterlily pools, 1957; 88" Longwood hybrid waterplatter measured by gardener William Pierson, 1979.

pounds apiece before collapsing. They are famous worldwide.

Yew topiary figures augmented the Sundial Garden in 1958, and an All-America Rose Garden was dedicated in 1959. A Rock Garden (renamed Hillside Garden in 1982) was designed and constructed by gardener Karl Grieshaber and Longwood staff in 1960 with a Heath and Heather Garden planted nearby in 1963. Routine garden maintenance continued through all this activity, including the moving of giant trees and the replacement of boxwood in the Main Fountain Garden after a 46" snowfall in March 1958.

Dr. Donald Huttleston, a taxonomist from the Brooklyn Botanic Garden, was hired in late 1955 to take on the daunting task of identifying, recording, and labeling thousands of plants. A dual system of labels for both public and staff use was devised. The response to a few trial lectures and classes in 1956 was so encouraging that an evening lecture series and short courses for the public were developed. Thousands of amateur enthusiasts and professional horticulturists have attended over the past 62 years.

Professional student training began in 1956 when the first International Student arrived from Denmark to work in the Gardens. A Summer Student program in conjunction with the University of Delaware began two years later. To support both students and staff, a specialized reference Library was established in 1956. Its current 35,000 items include not only Mr. du Pont's garden books but also the latest publications on botany, horticulture, landscape design, and garden history.

Director Seibert advocated a vigorous program of plant exploration and introduction to help make Longwood an internationally recognized public garden. In 1956, he and Walter Hodge initiated a collaborative agreement between Longwood Gardens and the USDA Agricultural

TOP: Moving Nordmann fir, 1956. BOTTOM: Dr. Donald Huttleston mounting herbarium specimens, c. 1958.

CLOCKWISE FROM TOP LEFT: Desert House labels, 1958; George Pring evening lecture in Ballroom, 1957; Annuals/perennials demonstration in Exhibition Hall, 1959; Library, 1965; Bulb Forcing class, 1959; Joseph Carstens teaching Summer Students about bonsai, 1962.

Dr. John Creech, USDA, at Longwood with chrysanthemum introductions from his 1956 plant exploration trip to Japan.

Research Service to explore areas not readily accessible. This led to 13 expeditions over the next 15 years that took Longwood and USDA explorers all over the world. Seibert also supported individual explorers collecting, for example, orchids in Burma in 1956, daturas in Colombia in 1956, and elms in the Himalayas in 1960. Seibert himself collected plants in South Africa in 1963, Peru in 1965, the Yucatan in 1967, West Indies in 1968, Costa Rica in 1969, and Honduras and El Salvador in 1971. Plants were also continually acquired as a result of staff travels and on 37 additional expeditions from 1984 through 2017.

Getting hundreds of new plants to Longwood from other American gardens or legally from overseas was just a first step. There had to be adequate facilities to grow everything needed for a prime horticultural display. In 1956 a plant Nursery and in 1958 an Experimental Greenhouse were established. A plant breeding program was initiated in 1960 under the direction of Dr. Richard Lighty. Additional production greenhouses were built in 1963.

Pierre du Pont formulated Longwood's aesthetic approach during his lifetime, aided by Mrs. du Pont and in later years by the head gardeners. After his death in 1954, some family members began to worry that although the Gardens were growing beautiful plants, some of the displays did not live up to the high standard which Pierre had always insisted upon. To address this concern the Trustees established in 1958 an Advisory Committee to help with aesthetic matters. One of the original participants was Pierre's second cousin Henry Francis du Pont (1880-1969), whose nearby Winterthur estate is a horticultural Mecca in its own right. Another member was Pierre's niece Wilhelmina du Pont Ross (1906-

CLOCKWISE FROM LEFT: Dr. Richard Lighty hybridizing delphiniums, 1964; The first Advisory Committee, from left, Genevieve du Pont, Henry Francis du Pont, Julia Bissell, H. Rodney Sharp, Wilhelmina du Pont Ross, 1965; David Paterson in Nursery propagation house, 1958.

2000), who took a passionate interest in Longwood's well-being. Since its founding, the Advisory Committe has played an integral role in maintaining the look and feel of Pierre du Pont's vision.

Besides the horticultural arts, the performing arts had a place in the new scheme, just as they had for Pierre du Pont. Clarence Snyder became organist on the retirement of Firmin Swinnen in 1956. The massive pipe organ in the Ballroom was rebuilt 1957-59 with a spectacular new console. Public organ concerts and evening musicales were regularly scheduled, and the Open Air Theatre was used more than ever. Summer evening displays of the famous Main Fountains were offered on a repeated basis beginning in 1956.

Even as the new Information Center opened in 1956, Dr. Seibert was already thinking about a larger visitor facility more in the geographic center of the Gardens. He had worked with the famed industrial design firm of Walter Dorwin Teague Associates on the American exhibit for the 1960 Floriade in Rotterdam. Subsequently for Longwood, Teague Associates created a modernist building cleverly covered on one side by a grassy berm and virtually invisible when viewed from inside the gardens. The barrel-vaulted Visitor Center opened in 1962 with a shop, auditorium, interpretive model, offices, and a 1,000-car parking lot on the site of the former golf course. At the same time an attractive stone-faced bridge was built over Route 1 to safely handle ever-increasing traffic.

By the mid 1960s, Longwood had been transformed from a magnificent private estate into an outstanding public garden, thanks to forward-looking Trustees who embraced the vision of Russell Seibert and his dedicated staff. But the transformation was far from finished.

LEFT: Möller organ console of bleached mahogany, 1959. OPPOSITE: Visitor Center, 1963.

1966-1976
Improvement

Palms were the most important group of tropical plants missing from Longwood's indoor displays up to the 1960s. Palm houses were traditional in European botanical gardens, but not at Longwood. Pierre du Pont preferred temperate houses because they were less expensive to heat, and only the small conservatory in the Peirce House was warm enough for an occasional palm. Drs. Seibert, Hodge, and Huttleston since 1956 had assembled a collection of about 100 species of palms, but there was no central place to display them. Finally, on Palm Sunday, 1966, the spacious Palm House opened with a landscape of 60 palms of all sizes and shapes best seen from an elevated walkway around the interior perimeter. The Palm House was designed by Victorine and Samuel Homsey, Inc., and was the last new public space added to the Conservatory; all subsequent display greenhouses have reused or replaced earlier structures.

Another new feature was the glistening Eye of Water modeled on the Ojo de Agua in Costa Rica, which Seibert had admired. Laminar flow hydraulic studies were made in 1966, and the surrounding shelter was designed by Homsey. It was inaugurated in 1968 and over the years the central Eye has been painted sky blue, Majorelle blue, brown, or black. It sits atop the underground reservoir formerly for the Main Fountains. As

OPPOSITE: Palm House, 1998. TOP RIGHT: Palm House, 1966. RIGHT: Eye of Water, 1998.

much as 5,000 gallons of water a minute overflow through the Eye, travel downstream, then crash over the Waterfall, only to be recirculated.

Other fountain work included an extension of the arched Pump House façade with its intricate carved wall fountains. Mr. du Pont had the westernmost 9 bays fabricated from metal trellis covered with vines arching over curved "sleigh" fountain basins. The free-standing trellis was removed in 1965. The architectural firm of Wason, Tingle, and Brust designed the building extension, which was finished by 1970. That was followed by a major re-plumbing of the Main Fountains from September 1970 until June 1972; almost 11,000 people visited on the day of the well-publicized final display before the 22-month fountain shutdown.

A wildflower garden and meadow had been contemplated for a number of years and in 1969 became a reality directly north of the Italian Water Garden. Famed mineralogist/botanist Dr. Edgar Wherry consulted on the project. The best wild species from within a hundred-mile radius were planted, offering woodland, pond, marsh, and meadow settings in close proximity. Also in 1969 at the suggestion of two county service organiza-

tions, a Perception Garden opened on a patio at the east end of the Information Center. It featured plants of different textures and scents planted at waist height, with printed and Braille labels; it was phased out 9 years later. A more permanent embellishment occurred in 1970 when an antique Italian carved stone wellhead was centrally placed in the Rose Arbor.

In 1971, the first room of the remaining 3-section nectarine house was converted to bonsai and the third room turned into a holding house for plants awaiting display. Four years later these houses were finally unlocked so that visitors could enter rather than just look in. The holding house became an educational display of container plants.

One project above all others took center stage. In 1967, the architectural firm of Richard P. Fox was retained to study the 1928 Azalea House, considered the "weak link" in Longwood display facilities because it required the most mechanical maintenance of any greenhouse. It was decided to substitute a free-span lamella arch roof, an "exciting departure from the more conventional greenhouse construction used previously here at Longwood," for the existing roof and columns. The potential for display

FROM LEFT: Main Fountain Garden Pump House before extension, 1965; Wellhead in Rose Arbor, 2001; Bonsai House, 1978. OPPOSITE: Managed Meadow, 1996.

would be much improved, especially by building additional greenhouses to supply the plants. Approximately 225 rhododendrons and azaleas from the old house were dug up, boxed, and moved into storage. Construction began in 1969 with hopes of finishing by late 1970, but the project was hampered by strikes affecting the contractors, and building dragged on until 1973.

The enormous Azalea House (now called the East Conservatory) with its great hourglass pathway opened with appropriate fanfare in April 1973. Adjoining it to the south were new indoor "Example Gardens" featuring pocket-sized "outdoor" gardens designed by regional landscape architects to suggest what the average visitor might have at home. In 1973 the theme was "Welcome to the Home - an Entryway"; in 1974 "A Service Area"; in 1975 "Patios"; and in 1976 "An 18th-Century Garden."

Longwood has always tried innovative techniques. In 1968 a trolley

FROM LEFT: Azalea House, 1973; The renamed East Conservatory, 1992.

rail was installed around the top interior perimeter of the Orangery and Exhibition Hall. From it a moveable gantry bucket is suspended so workers can safely trim the luxuriant creeping fig and bougainvillea growing up the columns that otherwise would engulf the Conservatory. In 1969 existing pumping equipment was converted into a snow-making machine to "mulch" the Heath and Heather Garden with a protective layer of snow. Later that year, a foam machine was used to spray outdoors mums in hopes of protecting them from light frosts. Both experiments were more trouble than they were worth, but they show the lengths to which Longwood will go to ensure quality displays. Other trials were made to enhance greenhouse plant growth by increasing carbon dioxide levels. More lasting has been, since 1971, soil sterilization in large containers using aerated steam, a technique developed in conjunction with Pennsylvania State University.

In 1970 because of new federal tax laws, the Longwood Foundation, Inc., became a charitable granting foundation. A newly chartered operating foundation, Longwood Gardens, Inc., assumed responsibility for the Gardens, with William H. Frederick, Jr., as president. Frederick was a

FROM LEFT: Snow machine, 1969; Director Russell Seibert, trustee William Frederick, Jr., landscape consultant Thomas Church, Maintenance head Arthur Jarvela, Horticulture head Everitt Miller, c. 1973.

landscape designer and nurseryman who brought horticultural experience to his appointment. Shortly thereafter, in March 1971, the celebrated California landscape architect Thomas Church (1902-1978) was engaged to advise on long-range planning, garden improvement, and visitor circulation. He designed two terraces for the Main Fountain Garden and the exterior approach to the new Azalea House, but his major contributions were to design the Theatre Garden (opened 1975) as a low-maintenance Mediterranean composition; the Wisteria Garden (1976) with tiered standards and an arbor; and the Peony Garden (1976) with tree peonies, Siberian irises, and golden-chain trees.

Two outstanding professional education programs were developed during this period. In 1967, the Longwood Graduate Program in Public Horticulture was born as a joint venture between Longwood and the University of Delaware. This was a dream of Russell Seibert and the University of Delaware's George Worrilow. Richard W. Lighty, Longwood's Geneticist, left his position at Longwood to become Program Coordinator at the University. Five graduate students each year received a 2-year

Fellowship to study the management of public gardens and earn a master's degree. From 1967 to 2017, more than 200 students participated, and many have had outstanding careers at arboreta, botanical gardens, community greening organizations, display gardens, and municipal beautification programs across the country.

In 1970, the Professional Gardener Training Program was launched, fulfilling Pierre du Pont's wish for a practical school of horticulture and floriculture at Longwood. The 2-year tuition-free program combines extensive hands-on gardening experience with classroom work for 8-10 new students, known as "PGs," per year. The program is highly regarded and has graduated more than 300 professional gardeners who are employed in public and private gardens, garden centers and nurseries, landscaping firms, and their own businesses.

When Dr. Richard Lighty left in 1967 to head the Graduate Program, Dr. Robert Armstrong replaced him as Geneticist and Plant Breeder. One of Armstrong's most important achievements was breeding impatiens hybrids from parents collected in New Guinea on a USDA-Longwood trip. Two of the hybrids were proudly displayed as a mass planting in the Azalea House in 1975. Dr. Seibert considered this the best example yet of Longwood's contribution to the world of new ornamental plants. Longwood released the hybrids to the horticultural industry in 1978 to the delight of home gardeners everywhere, who contiue to enjoy them in great numbers every summer. Another innovative concept was computerizing Longwood's 19,000 plant records in 1968 and 1969 as part of a pilot project at the American Horticultural Society. The effect of air pollution on ornamental plants was yet another area of interest, especially for the Director.

Russell Seibert had envisioned photography as an important way to let the rest of the world know about Longwood. Gottlieb Hampfler began at Longwood in 1934 as a gardener for Pierre du Pont and in 1955 he became Longwood's official photographer. His stunning pictures were supplemented with color movies made for public showings at Longwood and, by loan, to groups across the country. Two general movies (1961, 1966) and films on waterlilies (1964), orchids (1969), and chrysanthemums (1976) are now available on DVD.

History remained an important ingredient in the Longwood mix. In 1972, the Gardens were added to the National Register of Historic Places, the Nation's official list of cultural resources worthy of preservation. In 1976, the Peirce-du Pont House was opened for guided tours for 20,000 visitors, and two histories of Longwood were published. The United States was celebrating its 200th birthday and Longwood its 70th.

LEFT: Professional Gardener Trainee learns from William Rigler, 1971. OPPOSITE: Wisteria Garden, 2003.

1976-1986
Grand Pleasures

The imposition of a small admission fee in 1973 (the first since Sunday "hospital donation" fees were discontinued in 1954) was the catalyst for Longwood to reconsider its public image, especially as the 1976 U.S. Bicentennial approached. The Information Center had been designed when tickets weren't required; the shop kept most merchandise in glass cases. After much discussion with the Advisory Committee, architects Warren G. Hardwicke Associates gave a new look to the renamed Visitor Center in 1979. The original exposed façade was enclosed by a large addition with a classical feel. Design and Production, Inc., revised the orientation experience. An expanded self-service shop, facilities for processing groups, and a new multi-image theatre were added. An easily updated multi-image presentation replaced the movie that had been shown for a decade.

In the greenhouses, the honeycombed East Conservatory was slowly refined. Three "temporary" pools were installed in September 1977 as a central water feature, surrounded by holly trees and seasonal plantings. The adjacent Example Gardens changed from A Quiet Spot Featuring a Bench (1977) to Balcony Gardens (1978), Living with Plants (1980), then The Weekend Gardener (1984). The popular Orchid Display was comfortably enlarged in 1983 at the expense of the adjoining banana planting.

By 1977, Thomas Church could no longer visit because of declining health, and the noted English designer Sir Peter Shepheard (1913-2002) became Longwood's consulting landscape architect. His initial input was reflected in the landscape outside the new Visitor Center; in pathways around the Eye of Water, Waterfall, and Large Lake; in the eastern end of the Flower Garden Walk; in newly opened vistas, particularly around the Small Lake; and in grassy "islands" of the Managed Meadow.

Robert Armstrong led the Managed Meadow planning team beginning in 1978. Noted plantsman Hal Bruce advised on its plantings in 1979. Then in 1981, gardeners planted an "instant" deciduous hardwood forest of 15,000 seedling trees on 3 acres bordering the Meadow to screen staff housing from public view. An additional 4,350 trees were planted in 1983 to extend the belt in front of encroaching development. Favorable conditions ensured that almost too many trees survived. Beginning in 1985, periodic field burning rather than mowing was found to be the best way to control invasive species and to renew the Meadow.

Other refinements included recycling wood chips and composted leaf mold back into the Gardens for use as mulch on paths and in planting beds beginning in 1983. A new soil cropping program removed field soil from perimeter lands for greenhouse use, then spread compost made from the Garden's horticultural debris to rebuild field fertility for future use. An ongoing reevaluation of Longwood's overstocked plant nursery sent surplus to other public gardens. Plant records were computerized in-house for the first time in 1984-85. Integrated Pest Management, an environmentally conscious approach that uses the most effective yet least intrusive way to reduce the impact of pests and diseases, began in 1984. Electrical conservation had been practiced since the oil crisis of the 1970s, and in the 1980s greenhouse night temperatures were reduced and double-walled glazing was added to further conserve. Heating the greenhouse

OPPOSITE: Fireworks and Fountains, 2000.

soil (rather than the air) with buried pipes or cables was an even greater energy saver.

Not all horticultural news was happy, but change is inevitable in a mature garden. An enormous cucumber magnolia (shown in center background on page 17) dating from about 1800 next to the Peirce-du Pont House was infested with termites. The trunk was wrapped in plastic and fumigated, but to no avail. The tree had to be removed in 1978, but a cross-section was preserved for display. Also lost was Longwood's largest Kentucky coffee tree, equally as old, from behind the Open Air Theatre. In 1980, a 300-year-old white oak at the entrance dating from the time of William Penn was destroyed by high winds. Most distressing was the gradual decline from Dutch Elm Disease of Longwood's magnificent allée of American elms that framed a visitor's first view of the Gardens after the Visitor Center. The trees had been planted as mature specimens in the 1930s; a lovelier effect could not be imagined. The avenue was replanted with white oaks beginning in 1989, although one extraordinary elm has survived. In 1983, the hemlocks of Peirce's Park were sprayed from a helicopter to control the wooly adelgid insect and hemlock scale, a battle that

continues to this day. On a brighter note, First Lady Nancy Reagan presented Longwood with 3 National Landscape Awards from the American Association of Nurserymen in a ceremony at The White House on September 15, 1981.

In August 1979, Russell Seibert retired as Director after 24 years. He was succeeded by Everitt Miller (1918-2002), a commercial landscaper and retail florist who had managed the William Coe estate, Planting Fields, on Long Island before coming to Longwood in 1956 as chief horticulturist. In 1959 he became head of the Horticulture Department and was named Assistant Director in 1963. Miller was an enthusiastic public relations practitioner whose greatest achievement as director was spearheading the creation of Longwood's first restaurant.

The idea of offering refreshments dated back to 1927 when Pierre du Pont contemplated a produce stand/dairy bar to sell products from Longwood Farms, but the Depression and the lack of surplus killed that idea. The thought arose again in the late 1950s when the Information Center was planned, but it wasn't until 1979 that serious discussion began. The Terrace Restaurant, designed by Victorine and Samuel Homsey, Inc., opened in 1983 with both full and self-service dining just a few hundred feet from the Conservatory. The occasion was celebrated with a lavish Garden Party, the first since 1940, although guests now paid their own way. Subsequent galas have been held every few years.

The Restaurant was the most visible result of a new initiative to attract more visitors to the Gardens, an effort that began several years earlier. Lois Paul, who came to Longwood in 1960, had by 1963 reestablished Education as a priority following the 1961 departure of Walter Hodge.

LEFT: Trustee William Frederick, Jr., and landscape consultant Sir Peter Shepheard, 1981.

OPPOSITE: Suburban landscape in the Idea Garden, 1988.

Dr. Darrel Apps succeeded her in 1975 as Head of Education. A new focus on Visitor Education used fresh publications, better signs, and reinvigorated tours. A Children's Discovery Room was tried in 1979. The outdoor Idea Garden was reworked beginning in 1981 to increase Longwood's relevance to the average visitor with the latest in annuals, perennials, ground covers, grasses, roses, vines, herbs, berries, tree fruits, and vegetables. A suburban Food Gardening landscape by Rodney Robinson debuted there in 1982, an Herb Garden in 1984, and a small orchard planting in 1985.

Valuable publicity came with exposure on PBS's *Crockett's Victory Garden* in 1978 and in *Reader's Digest* in 1980. Photographers from all over the nation entered Longwood's first photo contest in 1979. Less educational but fun nonetheless were public bicycle rides in the Gardens from 1979 through 1983.

Employees and historians alike benefited from the efforts of gardener Dave Thompson, who in 1979 took over the editorship of the in-house *Longwood Chimes* newsletter. It had been first produced in 1957, but Thompson turned it into an extraordinary photographic chronicle of staff life and achievements. By 2012, a total of 288 issues had been published.

Longwood's full-time organist retired in 1978, and the position was replaced by a Performing Arts Coordinator, Audrey Baur. She and other staff members expanded programming mightily. In November 1981 the mum show became a month-long Chrysanthemum Festival built around an Asian theme, with crafts, exhibits, and performances. Attendance increased 30 percent, encouraging Longwood by 1983 to purchase its first TV advertising. Succeeding years featured fanciful themes like The Wonderful Garden of Oz, Where Dinosaurs Dwell, and Alice's Wonderland.

OPPOSITE: Chrysanthemum Festival in East Conservatory, 1997. RIGHT: Life-sized chrysanthemum dolls, 1999; Dinosaur topiaries, 1993.

Fantastic topiary figures graced many of the mum shows from 1984 to 2001. These were made from metal frameworks stuffed with sphagnum moss and covered with ivy, creeping fig, ferns, spider plants, and succulents. Subjects included life-sized elephants, giraffes, a carousel, 20-foot-tall pagoda, and 43-foot-long apatosaurus. In 2002 the focus shifted back to the arts of Asia, reconnecting the Chrysanthemum Festival to its oriental roots.

Chester County celebrated its 300th birthday at Longwood in 1982 with an 8-day Tricentennial Festival of the Arts. Beautiful weather and 150 events throughout the Gardens attracted 30,000 spectators.

By 1984 the celebratory festival concept included winter's Welcome Spring with indoor Fun Days for kids, and summer's Festival of Fountains with outdoor Ice Cream Concerts and performances before evening fountain displays. Fireworks with the fountains were first tried on Flag Day, June 14, 1980, to an audience of 3,000; these became so popular that pre-ticketing was necessary by 1985.

But nothing compared to the growth of Longwood's Christmas Display. In 1962, the display included 1,000 poinsettias indoors and a Christmas Tree Lane in the new parking lot for 6 days with the lighting of 3 evergreens and an 8-foot wreath for 2 hours each night. By 1978 that had grown to 74 outdoor trees with 40,000 lights. Evening choral concerts implemented in 1977 were supplemented by afternoon organ sing-alongs in 1978. For Christmas 1979, a first-ever decorated tree competition was held in the Ballroom, and a Victorian tree graced the never-before-opened Music Room. Attendance soared to 121,000, up from 70,000 the year before. In 1983, a renovated Colonial Village from Philadelphia's defunct Lit Brothers department store was exhibited in the Example Garden green-

house to a nostalgic public. By 1984, there were 81 trees outdoors with 60,000 lights, but safety concerns from so many cars prompted Longwood in 1985 to move the outdoor lighting from the parking lot into the Gardens proper. Christmas has grown steadily, with as many as 400,000 visitors in recent years enjoying an extravaganza of 500,000 lights, 200 concerts, dancing fountains, and superb floral displays.

In 1984, Everitt Miller retired and Frederick Roberts (b. 1942) became the new Director. Roberts earned a horticulture degree from the University of Connecticut and his master's in 1971 from the Longwood Program at the University of Delaware. He had directed Kingwood Center in Mansfield, Ohio, and the Worcester County (Massachusetts) Horticultural Society before returning to lead Longwood. His strong horticultural background, mechanical know-how, and public garden experiences were augmented by his appreciation for Longwood's early horticultural history, which had been his graduate thesis topic.

With attendance up and a new restaurant to feed the crowds, one might have expected the new Director to bask in Longwood's obvious success. But just below the surface there was more to do than ever.

OPPOSITE: Christmas at Longwood Gardens. ABOVE: Longwood Directors Everitt Miller (1979-1984), Frederick Roberts (1984-2006), and Russell Seibert (1955-1979) were photographed together in 1995.

1986-1996

The Art of the Garden

Fred Roberts brought to Longwood strong personal convictions formed over a lifetime of practical and managerial experience at all levels. The ultimate goal of the Trustees was to make Longwood the world's premier horticultural display garden, and Roberts felt this could be done through improved growing practices, the latest research techniques, inspired design, and the best possible maintenance of buildings and utilities. He worked hard to focus the entire organization on truly serving the visiting public.

The development of a philosophical approach to master planning was a priority. Landon Scarlett, who came to Longwood in 1969 as a gardener, began in 1973 to plan the displays for the new East Conservatory and, subsequently, other areas. She was named Coordinator of Planning and Design in 1985 and worked with the staff and Trustees to formalize a mission statement that was officially adopted in 1986:

Longwood Gardens is dedicated to preserving the spirit and beauty of the early twentieth-century gardens of Pierre S. du Pont. Longwood is a display garden promoting the art and enjoyment of horticulture for the public, while providing opportunities for research and learning. We are committed to excellence, good management, and fiscal responsibility.

LEFT: Mediterranean Garden, 2004. OPPOSITE: Orangery, 2003.

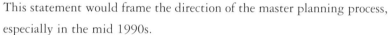

This statement would frame the direction of the master planning process, especially in the mid 1990s.

Even with just the beginnings of a master plan, new gardens were well underway. The greenhouse south of the East Conservatory that had housed the changing Example Gardens from 1973 to 1985 was transformed into a permanent Garden Path that opened in 1986. Reminiscent of the exuberant Acacia Path that bloomed annually in that location during Pierre du Pont's time, the Garden Path is a year-round tapestry of subtropical color, texture, form, and fragrance.

Pierre du Pont delighted in the company of his many young nieces and nephews, so it was appropriate that in 1987 an indoor Children's Garden opened in the former Container House next to the Garden Path. Designed by Catherine Eberbach as part of her Longwood graduate study, its tiny maze and interactive fountains were instantly adored by children of all ages. It was redesigned in 1990 and remained the most popular attraction for young visitors until closed in 2003. Its triple-sized replacement opened in late 2007.

Outdoors, the Waterlily Display was in need of reconstruction, and Sir Peter Shepheard was asked in 1987 to rework the original 1957 layout of 13 pools. He proposed only 5 brim-full pools with 30 percent more surface area, focusing attention on the sheets of water (as at Studley Royal in Britain, he noted) rather than on pool edges. The project was under construction in 1988 and opened the following summer with more than 100 types of day and night-blooming tropical waterlilies, hardy waterlilies, lotuses, giant waterplatters, and other aquatic and bog plants. Its summer palette of exotic colors is riveting.

One change that everyone noticed was the introduction in February 1989 of 9 tall *Washingtonia robusta* palms from Florida into the East Conservatory. These added a vertical drama that the house had always lacked. By 1996 the palms had grown so tall (some touching the roof) that they

were replaced by smaller specimens.

In 1985, the staff was reevaluating plant collections and thinking about rebuilding some of the smaller display greenhouses to rejuvenate structures as well as to create new visitor experiences. The 1921 greenhouse sheltering the 1958 Geographic House display was the first candidate. A completely new display was proposed, one that would allow more light and less heat into the adjoining Acacia Passage with its sun-loving, cool-temperature acacias. In 1986, Curator of Plants Rick Darke and Landon Scarlett spent 6 weeks in South Africa and took particular note of gray-foliaged plants of all kinds. Some were already featured in Longwood's Desert House, but not as the main elements in a designed landscape. Scarlett had been especially impressed by one such garden in Santa Barbara, California. Its designer, Isabelle Greene, had already worked on numerous West Coast gardens and was invited to consult on the Longwood project. In 1987, the tropical Geographic plants were given to the

Philadelphia Zoo, New York Botanical Garden, and United States Botanic Garden. Construction was underway in 1988. Massive rocks were placed by crane when the roof was temporarily off, with rock specialist Keir Davidson on hand to aid in the positioning. The new Silver Garden was completed by March 1989.

Longwood's Silver Garden recalls a dry desert stream bed, as if seen from an airplane, with enormous boulders and a river of slate. Its 150 taxa, or types of plants, total several thousand blue, gray, and silver specimens. Special root-zone heating permits cooler, less costly, winter air temperatures. It is a garden experience in the purest sense, a play of light and shade, structure and form, a work of art.

OPPOSITE, FROM LEFT: Garden Path, 1988; Children's Garden, 1998. ABOVE, FROM LEFT: Waterlily Display, 2004; Silver Garden, 1992.

The idea of a greenhouse display as an artistic work was next applied to the 1957 Desert House, whose plants had been incorporated into the Silver Garden. In 1988, Roberto Burle Marx (1909-1994) was asked to redesign the former Desert House, in conjunction with Philadelphia-based Conrad Hamerman. Brazilian Burle Marx was the most celebrated landscape designer of the twentieth century, and he already had visited and lectured at Longwood several times. In 1989, conceptual drawings were approved, and the following year detailed planting and construction plans called for a unique mix of stone, textural contrasts, water, and "exploding" columnar plantings mimicking palm trees. Longwood's staff traveled to Brazil in 1991, and plants were procured there and from

Florida and California. The new landscape was named the Cascade Garden (it has 16 waterfalls), and it opened in June 1992.

The Cascade Garden is an artistic expression of elements found naturally in the tropical regions of South America, where moist air and steamy earth erupt in lush foliage to fill every conceivable space. It is richly planted with 150 taxa, especially bromeliads and aroids. Tree-trunk-like columns covered with plants rise through the mist, filmy sheets of water cascade down rock channels, and colorful foliage sweeps along the curving path. Air plants cling to 35 tons of Pennsylvania mica, and 3,000 feet of heating cable keep tropical roots toasty during Pennsylvania winters.

In 1992, music-lover Burle Marx compared Longwood's many green-

houses to a symphony. The Cascade Garden, he noted, is a "crescendo, a finale to the experience."

But that finale was not the end to Longwood's perpetual striving for horticultural excellence. In 1990, a Mediterranean Garden was first proposed for the greenhouse of *Nepenthes* and food, fiber, and medicinal plants connecting the Orchid Display to the Palm House. In 1991, Rick Darke toured Australia and focused on its Mediterranean plants. Shortly thereafter Ron Lutsko, Jr., of San Francisco was chosen to design the garden. In

OPPOSITE, FROM LEFT: Gardener Rolfe Smith, Roberto Burle Marx, Conrad Hamerman planting the Cascade Garden, 1992; Cascade Garden, 1993. ABOVE: Mediterranean Garden, 1996.

December 1992, a tractor trailer hauled 700 plants from California growers to Kennett Square, and the garden was planted and opened in early 1993.

The 100-foot-long Mediterranean Garden celebrates the beauty and diversity of plants from the 5 Mediterranean-like regions of the world: parts of California, Chile, south and west Australia, South Africa, and the Mediterranean coast. Designer Lutsko references Renaissance and Islamic garden forms within greenhouse traditions peculiar to Longwood. Tiny pools collect water dripping from above and channel it to a central reservoir, recalling the precious rainfall of an arid climate. Stainless steel arbors allude to the greenhouse roof structure, while a steel bench shows new ways of using modern materials. The formal design is countered with

chaparral-like plantings that are loose yet luxuriant. The 90 different types of plants range from giant South African proteas, ixias, and kangaroo-paws to California arbutus trees, an Australian bottlebrush, and echiums from the Canary Islands. These have grown voluptuously in the pampered conditions of Longwood's greenhouse. Recent embellishments to the flora have amplified the blooming scheme and schedule.

The art of the garden was not limited to Longwood's Conservatory. Two million minor bulbs—geophytes—such as chionodoxa, crocus, muscari, and scilla were planted over a 20-year period starting in 1985 to create huge drifts of late winter color outdoors. Director Fred Roberts knew this could be a real crowd-pleaser and enlisted the Graduate Students to initially plan the display. Longwood's staff plants new areas periodically as the grand plan continues to evolve.

In 1989, the idea arose to populate Peirce's Park with gently colored native azaleas and rhododendrons, replacing the more garish exotics. A new distinction was made between the original arboretum (Peirce's Park) and the 7-acre pleasure park (renamed Peirce's Woods) to the southeast which runs down to the Large Lake. New paths were designed by Sir Peter Shepheard in 1990 and completed by 1992, and 350 native azaleas were readied in the Nursery. Some trees and shrubs were planted in 1993, but the biggest changes were planned in 1994-95 by consulting landscape architect W. Gary Smith who designed Peirce's Woods as an "art form" garden that brings together the most ornamental characteristics of the eastern deciduous forest. Thousands of native plants were added in 1995, including 10,000 rescued from the North Carolina mountains prior to impending highway construction. Under the high branches of oak, ash, maple, and tulip trees, sweeps of native shrubs and native ground covers carpet the woodland floor, punctuated by flowering understory trees. Named "rooms" (such as Cathedral Clearing) have been created within the Woods, with emphasis on fragrant native deciduous azaleas blooming from early spring to summer. The concept of using native plants to create a woodland garden as an art form is new to Longwood and one of the first such projects in any public garden.

There were two major restoration projects where the goal was not to create something new but to make sure that things looked as they always had, albeit incorporating the latest technology. Longwood's 1927 Italian Water Garden had water leaking from all the wrong places. After 3 years of planning, it was rebuilt from 1990 to 1992 and replanted to resemble its 1954 appearance. Pierre du Pont's original hydraulic calculations were found to be accurate when recalculated during the restoration, which substituted modern pumps and the latest computer controls.

Wayward water was also the impetus to rebuild Longwood's centerpiece, the Orangery and Exhibition Hall. Rainwater was seeping into the

OPPOSITE: Peirce's Woods carpeted in white tiarella and purple phlox, 1999. TOP: Geophyte plantings south of Rose and Topiary Gardens, 1998.

1921 structure, causing concrete to fall away from rusted steel. The roof glass was not shatterproof. Fertilizer water had corroded walkway grate supports and the utilities had grown chaotically. Reconstruction began in early 1995 with the removal of 3,500 cubic yards of soil in 10,400 loads. The roof was blasted with steel shot to remove paint, 260 tons of concrete were replaced, and 32 of 56 giant concrete columns were partially or totally remade. Below ground, 32 miles of pipe and conduit and 189 miles of wire were installed. The roof and windows were reglazed with 9,336 panes of glass weighing 38 tons. Replanted, the buildings opened in October 1996 looking as grand as ever.

Education remained a vital offering. Under Bill Thomas who replaced Darrel Apps in 1987, daily programs and useful printed information were geared more than ever to casual visitors. Plant society flower shows were expanded. For the Idea Garden, staff added new Annuals, Roses, Vines, and Groundcovers areas in 1987; sixty Ornamental Grasses in 1988; a Perennials area in 1991; and a Texture Garden in 1992. The Summer Laboratory which began in 1958 was phased out in 1986 (having hosted more than 300 college students in 28 years) and replaced by more flexible College Internships that had first been offered in 1982. An 8-week High School Internship program that brought Philadelphia students to work at Longwood began in 1995. The following year, a Groundskeeping Apprenticeship Program for local high school students was initiated, along with a horticultural career day for several hundred high schoolers from the entire region.

The Peirce-du Pont House evolved from guided tours in 1976 to self-guided visits by 1986. In 1992, the house was closed for major renovations and for the installation of the Heritage Exhibit, which opened on Longwood's 89th anniversary, July 20, 1995. The culmination of 7 years of planning and research, the Heritage Exhibit details Longwood's historical

FROM LEFT: Emptying Orangery beds of soil before rebuilding, 1995; Eupatorium, tulips, cytisus in Orangery, 2003; Ranunculus and muscari in Orangery, 2003. OPPOSITE: Peirce-du Pont House conservatory, 1996.

and horticultural legacy using period photos, letters, objects, and videos. Although the rooms housing the exhibit no longer were residential, their architectural features were preserved intact and are visible, as are photos in many rooms showing the decor during Mr. du Pont's occupancy.

Longwood ended its ninth decade with the satisfaction of knowing that major historic features created by Pierre du Pont had been successfully renovated with modern technology and looked as good (and as old) as ever. Congratulations were in order, too, for new indoor and outdoor landscapes that fused contemporary design to Longwood tradition.

Ten years away from a centennial…could there be anything left to do?

1996-2006
Grand Designs

During his first dozen years, Fred Roberts brought modern management techniques, improved business and investment practices, and the latest computer and communications technologies into all levels of the Longwood organization. A Trustee goal of generating on site half or more of the income needed to run the Gardens was met, especially in years when good weather boosted attendance. The condition of Longwood's buildings and utilities was improving, although an increased focus on safety uncovered less obvious areas in need of immediate improvement.

Longwood's full attention was now turned towards long-range planning. The thoughts of all interested parties as to how the Gardens should progress into the future were gathered and organized. Thirteen Principles (such as "Promote the art of horticulture" and "Demonstrate leadership in natural resource management") were developed to supplement the Mission and to guide the Gardens' activities and ethics. In 1996, W. Gary Smith and assistant Tres Fromme were hired to lead the planning process. In 1997 when Smith returned to the University of Delaware after a sabbatical, Fromme assumed the leadership role. By 2001, after intensive discussion among the entire staff and with community focus groups, *The Planning Vision* was published. It discussed 16 equally important issues critical to fulfilling Longwood's Mission and Principles: Heritage,

OPPOSITE: East Conservatory, 2005. RIGHT: Grapery in Estate Fruit House, 2006.

Horticulture, Design, Organizational Culture, Communication, Governance and Fiscal Responsibility, Safety and Security, Audiences, Visitor Experience, Learning, Performing Arts, Physical Plant, Transportation, Environmental Stewardship, Community Relations, and Perimeter Lands. Since the internal and external conditions affecting Longwood are not static, the plan continually evolves and, periodically, is rewritten to reflect this change.

Longwood's practice of the art and science of horticulture had some pioneering moments during the late 1990s. On November 19, 1998, a 10,100-pound sugar maple and an 8,100-pound copper beech were transported separately by helicopter from Longwood's perimeter to locations within the Gardens. These were not everyday transplant trees, but bare-root specimens with 20-inch trunk diameters and 35 to 40 feet tall. The beech eventually succumbed to poor drainage, but the sugar maple is quite content in its new home by the Open Air Theatre.

One problem for which there has been no simple solution is hungry deer. In 1989, a one-half-mile-long electric fence was first used to protect camellia trials. Beginning in 1998 employees have erected a 1,200-foot-long electric fence around the Flower Garden Walk *every night* from winter

FROM LEFT: Moving tree by helicopter, 1998; Production Greenhouse, 1999. OPPOSITE: Wetlands west of the Conservatory, 1998.

through early spring to protect shrubbery and bulb plantings. The fence is taken down the next morning before visitors arrive. In 1996, a 10-foot-tall barrier fence was installed around the expansive Nursery, but this is probably not a practical solution for the core Gardens.

A major leap forward was the 1999 opening of a 30,000-square-foot, state-of-the-art Production Greenhouse Facility sited north of the Waterlily Display. High-tech systems power the 378' by 80' range of 9 greenhouses, making it possible to produce exquisite plants year round under all conditions. Each greenhouse is equipped with its own computerized control system. The latest energy conservation techniques include root-zone heating to reduce air temperatures in winter and drawing in cooler air from adjacent woods in summer. Each house has two overhead curtain systems, one a 50-percent shade system and the other a blackout cloth system to eliminate all daylight for special crops or to lower the ceiling height to make it more efficient to heat or cool. In 2001, a mechanized soil mixing system was added to precisely combine up to 9 ingredients into one-yard increments of mixed growing medium which is then dispersed by an automatic pot filler.

Longwood's hidden infrastructure was improved, too. In 1997, an emergency generating plant was built to automatically activate a few seconds after a power failure. The generators can power the entire Gardens, including the fountains. Since Longwood is open many evenings, this adds to visitor safety. It also ensures that the Conservatory's critical control systems can function regardless of weather. Another enhancement invisible to visitors was the construction in 2001 of an underpass that permits Longwood vehicles to safely pass beneath a busy public road to get to a mainte-

nance complex on the northern edge of the Gardens. Like many projects this required the cooperation of township, county, and state officials.

Increased attention was given to the management of Longwood's perimeter areas not currently open to the public but critical to ensuring a protective greenbelt. These areas preserve the 19th-century agricultural landscape of once-rural Chester County as well as protect and recharge the watershed. In 1990 a Managed Wetland was proposed for a low-lying marshy area northwest of the Conservatory. The U.S. Fish and Wildlife Service sanctioned its design by Gary Smith in 1997 and planting started that spring. The wetland's primary purpose is to further purify water from runoff from the woods behind the Conservatory. Even more progressive is a huge pond where, since 1990, effluent from Longwood's wastewater treatment facility has been biologically purified before being sprayed over adjoining fields to naturally recharge the watershed rather than being dumped into local streams. The water is so pure that since 2009 all of it is used to irrigate the display gardens.

Education remained one of Longwood's strongest offerings. In 1996, planning began for the Red Lion Learning Community, a complex for the Gardens' resident students that could add to and enhance already existing housing, work areas, and student gardens. Construction was put on hold awaiting the Gardens' new master plan. The student programs saw changes in leadership with the retirement of David Foresman in 2000 after 30 years as Professional Gardener Training Program Coordinator. In 2005, Dr. Robert Lyons, former director of the JC Raulston Arboretum at North Carolina State University, succeeded Dr. James Swasey as the Graduate Program Coordinator. Swasey had overseen the Graduate Fellows since 1984.

Longwood's efforts to accommodate the general public resulted in some significant amenities. In 2000, motorized trams were added to help mobility challenged visitors, but these were replaced by individual electric scooters in 2003 that can go most anywhere. Audio wands from 2002 to 2008 gave visitors in-depth tours with commentary by the gardeners themselves; from 2008 to 2017, those stories were transmitted to personal cell phones. Front-line staff were reorganized into Visitor Services Associates, and the Visitor Center was modified yet again to create a more welcoming atmosphere, including a remodeled shop in 2005 and in 2008. Longwood's website was launched in 1997 and, with nearly two million

users annually, became the preferred way to learn more about the Gardens and its many programs.

An eighth seasonal festival was added to Longwood's horticultural year in 1995 with GardenFest, which highlighted the beauty of September and early October. The first year featured giant insect sculptures and a single weekend of activities. The season grew to a multi-week garden extravaganza that emphasized life at Longwood during the first half of the

OPPOSITE, FROM TOP: Cucurbit display, 2003; Orangery model and Garden Railway, 2002.
ABOVE: Lifting 62-bell carillon into Chimes Tower, 2001.

20th century. Outdoor displays ranged from antique cars and tractors to (beginning in 2000) a garden railroad that fancifully traveled to Longwood landmarks and important places in the lives of Pierre and Alice du Pont. Visitors enjoyed period music and old-fashioned garden games like badminton and croquet, while behind-the-scenes tours and a heritage trail focused on areas of historic interest.

Performing Arts continued as a major publicity generator and audience attractor. Priscilla Johnson became Performing Arts Coordinator in 1986 and, in addition to using the usual spaces, experimented with different types of programs in unexpected venues: Indian sitar music in the Italian Water Garden, Shakespeare excerpts from a Main Fountain Garden "balcony," modern dance choreographed for Peirce's Park—all utilized beautiful surroundings in novel ways. By the time Johnson retired in 2003, she had presented 6,366 performances to an audience of 2.3 million! Her successor, Dara Gordon Schmoyer, added depth to performing arts programming with activities to complete the visitor experience, including hands-on workshops, cultural cuisine, tie-ins with horticultural displays, and events that interpreted Longwood's history.

A significant performing arts addition was a new carillon for the 1930 Chimes Tower. Until 1956 it housed 25 tubular chimes that played old familiar melodies from punched paper rolls. From 1956 until 1981 electronic chimes with loudspeakers were used. In 2001, a 62-cast-bell instrument crafted in The Netherlands by Royal Eijsbouts and weighing 55,000 pounds was lifted by crane into the Tower. The carillon is played every day, either the traditional way by a live performer hitting large keys with the fists and feet, or automatically by computer.

Several other outdoor projects merit mention. In 2001, the famous allée of paulownia trees was replanted; fortunately the trees grew so fast that it took only a few years to recapture the majestic purple haze of its May bloom. In 2002, new paths were completed for a redesigned Forest Walk west of the Managed Meadow. In 2004, the Bee-aMazed Children's Garden opened in the Idea Garden with a Honeycomb Maze, Flower Fountain, and Buzz Trail. From autumn 2004 to autumn 2006, the Hillside Garden was redesigned by Tres Fromme to improve safety by simplifying its tortuous path system. To advise on these constant refinements, Douglas Reed from Reed Hilderbrand Associates in Massachusetts was named to succeed Sir Peter Shepheard as consulting landscape architect in 2002, continuing a tradition dating back to Thomas Church in 1971. Reed worked with Longwood until early 2006.

But the grandest designs were reserved for indoors. The reconstruction of the eastern third of the Conservatory led to a flurry of greenhouse swapping. In 1998, the staff proposed expanding the existing indoor Children's Garden into the neighboring Nectarine and Bonsai Houses, but those displays would have to move elsewhere. The espaliered nectarine and indoor grape displays were transferred to the newly named Estate Fruit House which opened in 2002. The 3-section garden was designed by

OPPOSITE: Hillside Garden, 2003. ABOVE: Hillside Garden after redesign, 2008.

Tres Fromme with assistance from fruit grower Mary Allinson to creatively reuse an existing 1921 greenhouse. The 140' by 27' Fruit House is, essentially, a sculpture garden of changing patterns of light and shadow within the bold structure of formally trained nectarine trees, grape vines, and melon plants, along with lemons, pomegranates, figs, and other fruits and vegetables. Historical photos and interpretive text tell of Pierre du Pont's passion for growing fresh produce under glass. Fruit is produced at least a month ahead of the outdoor season by controlling heating and ventilation. A mature nectarine tree can yield about 200 nectarines every year; each vine, about 12 bunches of grapes.

Also in 2002 the new Bonsai House opened in an equally old greenhouse. Floriculturist Sharon Loving led its conversion to a display area with removable glass panels that permit the plants to be seen but kept cold and dormant during the winter. Bonsai caretaker Mary Allinson designed the display benches to best showcase as many as 15 of Longwood's 40 bonsai at any one time.

Without a doubt, the major effort of Longwood's tenth decade was the redesign of the 1973 East Conservatory, which had always been plagued by poor ventilation and a leaky roof. Few projects had a longer gestation. In 1985, when the issue was first raised, Roberto Burle Marx gave his opinions on the interior landscape possibilities. Ventilation was improved somewhat in 1987, but the roof still leaked. In 1989, Sir Peter Shepheard and structural engineer Nicholas Giannopulos proposed a new single-span roof design with a tall center peak. This metamorphosed a half dozen times until in 1997 a ridge-and-furrow roof (akin to the original 1928 roof but having a central monitor like Longwood's Orangery) with 9 pairs of interior columns was chosen.

LEFT, FROM TOP: Melons in Estate Fruit House, 2004; Nectarines in Estate Fruit House, 2004; Bonsai House, 2006. RIGHT: East Conservatory, 2006.

CLOCKWISE, FROM FAR LEFT: Views of East Conservatory, with yellow clivias, 2007; Panorama looking east, 2008; Red begonias and aechmeas, 2009; Looking west from entrance, 2006; View east across pool, 2006.

For the landscape, a 1995 design competition with 60 entries from 4 design schools opened Longwood's eyes to all possibilities. A professional design firm was engaged in 1997 and replaced by another in 2000, but in 2001 the interior design was turned over to Tres Fromme, Longwood's Planning and Design Leader, assisted by Sharon Loving and other key staff. The half-acre garden under a 52-foot-high roof is a grand landscape that unfolds in a series of unique spaces recalling Moorish, French, and Modernist influences. Shifting views, exquisite forms and textures, and delicious fragrances engage the senses. Mediterranean and subtropical flora complement large displays of seasonal blooming plants. Water in streams, flat sheets, falls, and jets adds motion, reflection, and sound. A Court of Palms, Patio of Oranges, and Court of Bamboo provide places to linger or enjoy performances. Construction began in 2003 and finished in time for Longwood's 2006 Centennial, officially opening on October 29, 2005.

Concurrently the Music Room and Ballroom were closed 2001-2005 for massive reconstruction to replace leaky roofs and outdated utilities, expand service areas, install an organ exhibit, and restore the exquisite interior decoration. The Music Room ceiling reclaimed its original luster, the Ballroom received a new walnut parquet floor, and the walls of both rooms were hung with freshly loomed rose-colored damask.

OPPOSITE, FROM TOP: Rose Arbor Concert, 2006; Longwood's Staff on July 20, 2006, the Gardens' 100th birthday. RIGHT: Restored Ballroom with Pierre du Pont's 1930 mahogany table set for 60 dinner guests, 2006. The table extends to 72' 8" and can seat 76.

These many projects came to fruition in time for Longwood's centennial celebration during 2006. An entire year of special activities highlighted a century of excellence and innovation in horticulture, education, preservation, and philanthropy. In January, a 20 by 40-foot walk-in exhibit reminiscent of the Conservatory was staged at the week-long Pennsylvania Farm Show in Harrisburg. Longwood's birthday, July 20, was celebrated on site with a group photo of the entire staff, a giant cake shaped like the Conservatory, an evening concert by the Kennett Symphony of Chester County performing the world premiere of *The Century Garden* by Robert Maggio with 3 movements entitled *Trees / Flowers / Fountains*, and fireworks; 2,000 attended that day, with 11,600 for the official 3-day celebration. Two months later, 33 plant explorers assembled to reminisce about their 50 years of plant collecting on behalf of Longwood and to celebrate the publication of Tomasz Anisko's *Plant Exploration for Longwood Gardens*, a 334-page chronicle of 50 expeditions to 30 countries; the book was accompanied by an extensive exhibit. One can only imagine how pleased Pierre du Pont would be that his purchase of Peirce's Park on July 20, 1906, and his subsequent efforts would be celebrated 100 years later with such gratitude and enthusiasm.

LEFT: The Kennett Symphony of Chester County performing *Fountains* from *The Century Garden* by Robert Maggio on Longwood's 100th birthday, July 20, 2006.

2006-2106

The Next Century

Longwood's third director, Fred Roberts, retired on July 16, 2006, after 22 years of service. Paul B. Redman began the next day as the Gardens' fourth director. Redman was born in Texas and raised on an Oklahoma ranch. He received bachelor's and master's degrees in horticulture from Oklahoma State University and worked at Hawaii's National Tropical Botanical Garden before moving to the Franklin Park Conservatory in Columbus, Ohio, as Horticulture Director in 1995 and, ultimately, as Executive Director in 1997. After 10 years at Longwood, his director's title was changed to President and CEO in 2016, and other key staff were retitled Vice Presidents, Directors, or Managers of their various divisions.

Longwood's change in leadership was followed by a new focus on decentralized empowerment, marked by periodic "Town Hall" meetings where several hundred employees, students, and volunteers come together to share job-related victories both large and small, and where everyone partakes of the same overviews as given to the Board of Trustees. The Board was gradually enlarged to 18 members by 2017 and asked to take a more expansive role, particularly in visionary master planning.

ABOVE: Paul Redman became Longwood's fourth director in 2006. RIGHT: The rebuilt Main Fountain Garden at full display, 2017.

LEFT: The Meadow Garden amid morning mist, September 2015.

That process was facilitated by Lord Cultural Resources, an international consulting firm, and began in earnest in 2008 with a comprehensive self-examination and by evaluation of other gardens from around the world. As a result, a new Mission Statement, answering the question "Why do we exist?," was approved in February 2009: *Longwood Gardens is the living legacy of Pierre S. du Pont, inspiring people through excellence in garden design, horticulture, education, and the arts.* A new Vision for the institution states: *Longwood Gardens is one of the great gardens of the world. We strive for innovation in horticulture and display. We present the arts in an unparalleled setting to bring pleasure and inspire the imagination of our guests. We contribute to society through excellent and diverse education programs, horticultural research, environmental stewardship, and cultural and community engagement.* Core values were identified as: excellence through innovation, creativity, experimentation, and professional development; advancement of public horticulture through global leadership; sound financial practices; conservation and sustainability; and being relevant, accessible, and welcoming to all.

Short-term (2010-2015, 2016-2022) Strategic Plans set specific goals and tasks to support the advancement of the new vision, and a long-term Facilities Master Plan compiled a wish-list of ideal facilities. An Interpretive Strategy established the concept and complexity of "beauty" through which visitors can have an extraordinary guest experience. A Heritage Management Plan proposed a strategy for the care and conservation of collections and historical resources. A Brand Plan established how Longwood portrays and communicates itself to the rest of the world. A massive Landscape Evolution Report, compiled by Heritage Landscapes LLC, documented the physical history of the entire property, revealing that the one

constant is change. The most successful gardens are always in motion, and Longwood is no exception, yet while the Gardens have evolved as an organization, the founding spirit of change, innovation, and excellence remains untouched.

The final phase of the initial planning effort, which drew upon all the other plans, was a 40-year Site Landscape Master Plan that was developed in 2010-2011 with the help of West 8, an award-winning Dutch urban design and landscape architecture firm. West 8 worked with architects, designers, civil and environmental engineers, artists, and other specialists from around the world to suggest how to expand yet unite the Longwood experience, provide a more centralized route for pedestrian traffic, and relocate some operations to the outskirts of the property. Also considered were the evolving needs of guests and of participants in Longwood's educational programs and ways to develop the technological infrastructure of the Gardens. The resulting concepts are invaluable to present-day and future stewards of the institution.

ABOVE: The Meadow Bridge, with two levels, artfully curves across a slight ravine, August 2015. RIGHT: Mirrored Hourglass Lake in late afternoon, November 2017.

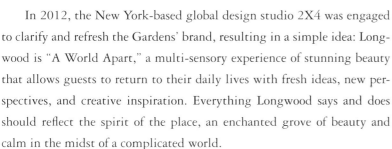

In 2012, the New York-based global design studio 2X4 was engaged to clarify and refresh the Gardens' brand, resulting in a simple idea: Longwood is "A World Apart," a multi-sensory experience of stunning beauty that allows guests to return to their daily lives with fresh ideas, new perspectives, and creative inspiration. Everything Longwood says and does should reflect the spirit of the place, an enchanted grove of beauty and calm in the midst of a complicated world.

Redman also redefined Longwood's organizational structure to improve the guest experience and to make best use of innovative 21st-century technology. The Horticulture and the Maintenance Departments had already been augmented in 2003 by splitting the third department, Administrative Services, once again into two stand-alone departments, Administration and Education. In 2007, two new departments were created by reassigning staff: Guest Services (charged with defining how to deliver excellent customer service, and handling all aspects of visitors'

experiences from ticketing and safety to wayfaring, learning, and performing arts to dining and shopping) and Marketing. An Information Technology division was formalized in 2007 and incorporated into Maintenance in 2010, which was subsequently renamed the Facilities Department. This gave Longwood six departments with 242 full-time personnel, 383 part-time, 200 contractual, 41 students, 25 to 100 seasonals, and 800 volunteers, totaling more than 1,700 individuals by 2018.

Thematic programming for an entire year took on new importance. In 2006, all activities revolved around Longwood's Centennial. In 2007, the eight long-standing seasonal festivals (Welcome Spring, Easter, Acres of Spring, Festival of Fountains, GardenFest, Autumn's Colors, Chrysanthemum Festival, and Christmas) were condensed into five (Winter Escape, Spring Blooms, Festival of Fountains, a greatly expanded Autumn's Colors /Chrysanthemum Festival, and Christmas), although the offerings were just as comprehensive. A three-day orchid show and sale in 2007 grew to a

OPPOSITE: Exhibition Hall orchids on columns encircled by curtains of falling water, 2008. ABOVE, FROM LEFT: Orchid Meadow in East Conservatory, 2014; 12-foot-tall Orchid Arch covered with more than 600 yellow and white *Phalaenopsis* orchids in the East Conservatory, 2018.

two-month-long exhibit in 2008, which was so popular with visitors that Winter Escape was renamed Orchid Extravaganza the following year and continues to attract nearly 100,000 visitors.

2008 was built around *Nature's Castles*, three extraordinary wooden tree houses that opened in April: a 20-foot-high Birdhouse, a Lookout Loft reminiscent of Adirondack-style *art nouveau*, and a two-story Canopy Cathedral inspired by a Norwegian church. Designed by acclaimed specialists from Vermont and Washington State and built to be environmentally friendly, the "temporary" structures were so popular that they became permanent additions. *The Buds & the Bees: Pollination and the Secret Lives of Plants* was the 2009 theme, partially inspired by and featuring the groundbreaking hummingbird photography of former trustee Crawford Greenewalt (1902-1993) and highlighted by four giant wood sculptures of a hummingbird, butterfly, and bees by artist David Rogers, and by a glass-walled working bee hive for summer display. 2010 featured *Making Scents: The Art and Passion of Fragrance*, an exhibit capped by the release of *Always in Bloom*, a signature fragrance built around lily-of-the-valley and created by celebrated *parfumeur* Olivier Polge.

A Wonder in Every Sense promoted the sounds of Longwood for 2011, highlighted by the completion of a multi-year, $8.7 million restoration

LEFT, FROM TOP: David Rogers' wood Hummingbird in the Idea Garden celebrated pollination, 2009; Bee topiaries buzzed the Orangery, 2009. OPPOSITE, CLOCKWISE FROM TOP LEFT: Canopy Cathedral overlooking Large Lake, 2008; View from Canopy Cathedral, 2008; Birdhouse near Peirce-du Pont House, 2009; Lookout Loft overlooking Meadow, 2010. This last was designed by Forever Young Treehouses, Burlington, VT; the first two were by Treehouse Workshop, Seattle, WA. All use innovative pin foundations to safeguard the living tree roots.

of the Gardens' most historic musical asset, the 10,010-pipe Aeolian Organ dating from 1929. First-ever climate control and an innovative mist fire suppression system ensure state-of-the art preservation. A new four-manual computerized console with 353 tilting tablets resembles the original but is infinitely more flexible. The space surrounding the organ was transformed into a permanent exhibit telling the history of the organ. Hands-on working models show how it operates, and floor-to-ceiling glass windows offer a close-up look at more than 5,000 of its pipes. Planning began in 1997, the new console arrived in 2001, and the exhibit opened in 2005, but it took from 2004 to 2011 to restore the instrument, culminating with a gala recital by famed Wanamaker organist Peter Richard Conte in February 2011; tonal finishing and adjustments continued into 2013. Both the organ and Pierre du Pont's 1923 Steinway grand piano (restored in 1979 and 2009) can now be heard almost daily, thanks to computers that recreate both historic and recent performances on the actual instruments.

The Steinway grand was itself the subject of a special six-month 2011 exhibit in the Music Room entitled *Notes from the Forest* that delved into the story of musical instruments made from wood. The creation of a Steinway piano was fully explored, honoring the International Year of the Forest as declared by the United Nations General Assembly to raise awareness of sustainable forest management around the globe.

For 2012, Longwood commissioned a British fiber-optic artist to present a garden-wide exhibition, *Light: Installations by Bruce Munro*, from June through October. Munro is best known for immersive large-scale lighting projects, and he didn't disappoint with six huge outdoor and two indoor installations. There were 27,000 illuminated stems that glowed like bioluminescent spheres, 235 miles of optic fiber, 17,388 recycled plastic bottles

OPPOSITE: The 2001 organ console resembles the 1929 Aeolian console. ABOVE: 17,388 recycled bottles were transformed into illuminated *Water Towers* for *Light* in 2012, accompanied by a variety of music in the Meadow.

FROM LEFT: *Snowballs* were six color-changing glass chandeliers hanging in the Orangery; *Light Shower* had 1,650 teardrop diffusers suspended in the Exhibition Hall and reflected in the flooded floor; *Forest of Light* comprised 20,000 illuminated glass spheres reminiscent of seeds bursting into bloom after a rainfall. All from *Light: Installations by Bruce Munro*, 2012.

stacked into 69 glowing towers, and 65,000 recycled CDs transformed into waterlilies floating on the Large Lake. The after-dark spectacle dazzled almost 300,000 visitors.

Beyond the Garden Gates for 2013 offered a fascinating look at all aspects of the work spaces, staff, inspiration, and ingenuity that make up Longwood, proving that what's behind the scenes is also a thing of beauty. Guests interacted with staff as never before, and online blogs and videos were a powerful means to communicate. *Secrets of Victoria: Waterlily Queen* was a special summer-long exhibit in the Music Room celebrating the unique beauty of one of Longwood's signature plants, *Victoria* waterplatters and their hybrid offspring that are the centerpiece of the outdoor waterlily display. Old and new photographs, lithographs, books, and video focused on the haunting history of these celebrated aquatics. The exhibit accompanied a new book on the topic by Tomasz Aniśko.

Roots celebrating Longwood's connections to the land, community, and history was the overarching theme for 2014. An outdoor exhibit marked the 100th anniversary of the Open Air Theatre, with a Walk of Fame featuring bricks named for artists who had performed there. The high point of the year was opening the reimagined Meadow Garden, first conceived in 1969 but now expanded to 86 acres after relocating busy highway Route 52 that bisected the property. Redesigned by Jonathan Alderson and Longwood staff, the Meadow's mowed and gravel paths, elevated walkways, wooden interpretive pavilions, and pleasing bridges permit visitors to make their way on foot to a distant 1730-era Quaker farmhouse, now an interpretive center. The Meadow Garden's themes explore such concepts as history of the land, Longwood's heritage of preserving open spaces for the public, land stewardship, and natural beauty, variety, and inspiration.

OPPOSITE, CLOCKWISE FROM TOP: *Field of Light* featured 7,000 color-changing frosted glass spheres at the Small Lake; *Arrow Spring* wove 15,000 points of light into a meandering stream of planted sage; *Field of Light* close-up, 2012

ABOVE, FROM TOP: Glass pumpkins by Michael Cohn and Molly Stone in Music Room, 2008; *Secrets of Victoria: Waterlily Queen* exhibit in Music Room, 2013

Concurrently, an inaugural Longwood Community Read brought together a diverse audience of staff, guests, local and regional schools, libraries, and conservation organizations to discuss Aldo Leopold's *A Sand County Almanac*, exploring Leopold's "land ethic," ecological restoration, and natural land preservation ideas using the Meadow Garden as a contextual framework. The Meadow Garden continues to provide an opportunity

ABOVE: Indian Hannah memorial in new location near entrance gates, 2016. OPPO-SITE: Silver Garden installation for *Nightscape* with undulating waves of blue, green, purple, and turquoise projections, 2015.

for guests to visit a managed natural Piedmont landscape and showcases sensitive land stewardship techniques that blend horticulture and ecology.

The relocation of Route 52 closed public access to a large upright stone marker with a bronze plaque placed in 1925 by the Pennsylvania Historical Commission and the Chester County Historical Society on that road's eastern shoulder about 1,200 feet from the Route 1 intersection. The monument marked the nearby c. 1730 birthplace of "Indian Hannah" Freeman, a Native American who in 1925 some considered "the last of the Lenni-Lenape or Delaware Indians," although in truth she was not the last. It was relocated in 2014 to a much more prominent position just north of the Longwood Meetinghouse across from Longwood's entrance and rotated to point towards the valley where Hannah was supposedly born. It was rededicated that May, with officials recreating the 1925 dedication photo.

Rebuilding the Main Fountain Garden from late 2014 into 2017 could have discouraged visitation in 2015 and 2016, but that was not the case. While *New Heights: The Fountain Revitalization Project* was the underlying theme around which exhibits and presentations were built, attention focused on a two-summer spectacular entitled *Nightscape: A Light and Sound Experience* by Klip Collective. Ricardo Rivera and his Klip colleagues from Philadelphia designed site-specific installations that projected colorful, digitally mapped, abstract videos onto plants, especially mature trees and forest walls. Outdoors, giant kaleidoscopes and flying fish lit up the eastern gardens. Indoors, projections glittered up the East Conservatory, Exhibition Hall, Palm House, and Silver Garden. Newly composed music throughout capped a truly unique experience that filled the summers and autumns of 2015 and 2016 with 335,000 specially ticketed visitors.

On a smaller scale but impressive in its own way was the addition of after-dark Luminaries for six nights during the summer of 2017. Inspired by illuminations of European gardens such as at Vaux-le-Vicomte in

OPPOSITE, CLOCKWISE FROM TOP LEFT: *Nightscape* projections down Flower Garden Drive; Projection on *Bismarckia nobilis* palm in Rose Arbor; Immense dragonfly projected onto Large Lake woods.

ABOVE, CLOCKWISE FROM TOP: Large Lake projections; Digital images on topiary danced to unique electronic music; Silver Garden projections; all 2015 or 2016.

France, Longwood staff and volunteers placed nearly 3,000 real candles in rigid bags to create geometric designs throughout the landscape. The Cow Lot and areas along the Flower Garden Walk were featured in August, and the Lakes and Italian Water Garden were illuminated in September. More than 32,000 guests enjoyed the spectacle. Future evenings are planned.

Multi-generational activities have been programmed at Longwood since the 1980s, but in recent years the offerings have been more closely connected to seasonal and interpretive themes. Offerings over the past decade complemented special exhibitions such as *Making Scents*, and *Light*. Seasonal programs such as *OrKID Days* during Orchid Extravaganza, *Meet Us in the Meadow* which encourages guests to explore the Meadow Garden and introduces the preservation of native habitat, and *Night of 1000 Lights* with lanterns and Asian music during the Chrysanthemum Festival attracted between 1,000 and 3,000 guests each time.

LEFT AND ABOVE: More than 2,100 luminaries (real candles in rigid containers) outlined the Italian Water Garden for three nights in September 2017.

Excellence in all the arts is important to Longwood's mission, and beginning in 2006 Performing Arts expanded its scope by presenting nationally and internationally known classical, jazz, and pop artists. Performers ranged from Marc Cohn and Shawn Colvin in 2006; Gaelic Storm in 2007; Kenny Garrett, Sophie Milman, Susan Tedeschi, Derek Trucks in 2008; Bill Charlap, Shemekia Copeland, Taylor Eigsti, Eileen Ivers, Julian Lage, Boz Scaggs, McCoy Tyner, Rufus Wainwright (*taped for TV) in 2009; to the Ahn Trio*, Joan Armatrading, Terence Blanchard, Chris Isaak, B.B. King, and Jane Monheit in 2010.

When Tom Warner, former Vice President of Programming at Philadelphia's Kimmel Center, joined the staff in 2011 as Director of Performing Arts, the offerings expanded even further in number and variety, with a series showcasing musical artists from around the world in addition to the

ABOVE: 601 upside-down parasols created a colorful ceiling in the Exhibition Hall for the 2011 Chrysanthemum Festival. RIGHT: 500 floating lanterns in the Exhibition Hall marked a *Night of 1000 Lights* during the 2015 Chrysanthemum Festival.

jazz, organ, and classical artists already appearing. The Beach Boys, Regina Carter, Kurt Elling, Gipsy Kings, Bruce Hornsby, Indigo Girls*, King's Singers, Keb' Mo'*, Pink Martini, Mavis Staples, Australia's Strange Fruit, and Suzanne Vega appeared in 2011. The Bacon Brothers, Barbara Cook, Vince Gill, Manhattan Transfer*, Pat Metheny Unity Band, Anoushka Shankar*, Soledad Barrio & Noche Flamenca, Soweto Gospel Choir, and Straight No Chaser visited in 2012. Pat Benatar, Tony Bennett, Dervish, Amy Grant, Buddy Guy, Ladysmith Black Mambazo, Lyle Lovett, Michael McDonald, Molly Ringwald, Ukelele Orchestra of Great Britain, Vienna Boys Choir, and Peter Yarrow & Noel Paul Stookey all performed in 2013. The Canadian Brass, Rosanne Cash, Savion Glover, Jazz at Lincoln Center

with Wynton Marsalis, and Patti LuPone visited in 2014 along with Max Raabe & Palast Orchester, and the Venice Baroque Orchestra. In 2015, BalletX, Danu, Melissa Etheridge, Hugh Masakela, Oliver Mtukudzi*, New York Voices*, Orquesta Buena Vista Social Club, Philadanco, Philly POPS, Pine Leaf Boys*, Sweet Honey in the Rock, and Le Vent du Nord brought their talents to the Gardens. Altan, Chick Corea, Natalia Lafourcade*, Yo-Yo Ma and the Silk Road Ensemble, Taj Mahal, Mnozil Brass, the Swingles, and Pablo Ziegler all appeared in 2016; and in 2017 Monty Alexander, Sergio & Odair Assad, Kenny Barron, DakhaBrakha, Bela Fleck, Kathy Mattea, Natalie Merchant, Cristina Pato, Farah Siraj, and Julieta Venegas* performed for enthusiastic crowds.

ABOVE: The Taj Mahal Trio and Bettye LaVette rocked the Open Air Theatre in 2016.

OPPOSITE: The Exhibition Hall provided a memorable backdrop for a 2016 concert by Time for Three.

The Philadelphia PBS station WHYY starting taping concerts at Longwood in 2009 for a half-hour *On Tour* television series and by 2017 had captured 11 concerts for broadcast, identified above * by an asterisk. For Christmas 2014, PBS presented youthful singer Jackie Evancho in *Awakening—Live in Concert*, taped that August in a dramatically decorated Open Air Theatre that aired nationwide several times over two years.

Professional ice skaters added a unique element to the Christmas display from 2006 through 2009 on a frozen rink in the Pear-Shaped Basin beneath the Chimes Tower. An annual Wine & Jazz Festival began in May 2007, with 200 types of wine, day-long live music, and as many as 5,200 attendees. Wine & Jazz headliners have included Jon Batiste, DeeDee Bridgewater, Branford Marsalis, John Pizzarelli, Dianne Reeves, and Arturo Sandoval.

Philadelphia's famed Curtis Institute of Music performed in the Gardens in 2008, and a partnership was announced in 2009 bringing instrumental and voice recitals, orchestral concerts, and master classes; one highlight in 2009 was Vivaldi's *Four Seasons* played live in the Exhibition Hall with high-definition projections showing the seasons at Longwood. That same year Longwood began presenting outstanding classical pianists, including Di Wu

(2009), Haochen Zhang (2010), Olga Kern (2011), Stewart Goodyear (2011), Simone Dinnerstein (2011 and 2017), Daniil Trifonov (2013), Andre Watts (2013), Vadym Kholodenko (2014), Valentina Lisitsa (2014), and Yefim Bronfman (2016). Visiting artists were shared with local colleges for master-classes, such as violinist Mark O'Connor, the string trio Time for Three, and jazz pianist Danilo Perez. Orchestral concerts in 2012 included the Baltimore Symphony Orchestra and in 2017 the Delaware Symphony, with pianist Peter Serkin, and the Havana Lyceum Orchestra from Cuba, with soloist Simone Dinnerstein.

In 2009, Longwood welcomed the 67th Congress of the Guild of Carillonneurs in North America with 130 bell aficionados from all over the world. In 2017 a Carillon Festival featured 12 solo and duo recitals (some in combination with other instruments and a vocalist). Longwood is hosting the World Carillon Federation World Congress in 2020 with bell enthusiasts from around the globe.

With its spirit of innovation, Longwood has also commissioned new works, including *Lost in the Meadow*, a 2015 site-specific play created in conjunction with the regional People's Light theatrical company. Set out-doors in the 86-acre Meadow Garden, the piece required the audience to wear wireless headphones to hear actors that appeared as tiny specks hun-dreds of feet away. *Tall Tales on the High Seas* was a 2017 commissioned production by the circus/dance troupe Australia's Strange Fruit, with pole-bending acrobatics and an instrumental/vocal soundtrack enhanced by live carillon bells. A chamber work by pianist and composer Michael Brown debuts in 2018.

OPPOSITE: Australia's Strange Fruit fascinated audiences with its acrobatic *Tall Tales on the High Seas* production in 2017. ABOVE: Wine & Jazz Festival between Peirce's Park and Meadow, May 1, 2010.

The Longwood Organ remains a major arts contributor, especially with the appointment of Peter Richard Conte, Wanamaker Grand Court Organist at Macy's Philadelphia, as Principal Organist in 2012. Recitals have been given by world-renowned organists, including Steven Ball, Cameron Carpenter, Ken Cowan, Isabelle Demers, Felix Hell, Paul Jacobs, Olivier Latry, Nathan Laube, Alan Morrison, James O'Donnell, Hector Olivera, Nigel Potts, Jean-Baptiste Robin, and Daniel Roth. Particularly noteworthy was the first periodic International Organ Competition in 2013 with contestants from around the world vying for the $40,000 PS du Pont First Prize. UK native Benjamin Sheen from Julliard won in 2013, and American Joshua Stafford from Curtis and Yale won in 2016.

In 2017, the Longwood Organ Academy was established as a week-long summer residence program for college students pursuing degrees in organ performance. Students study the increasingly popular art of transcribing orchestral music using the Longwood instrument, one of the world's great symphonic organs. Coached by Peter Richard Conte and the Curtis Institute of Music's Alan Morrison, participants also have master classes with other prominent organists and inspect some nearby instruments, notably the Wanamaker Organ in Philadelphia. The Academy concludes with a Longwood recital given by all the students. The week is a thrilling learning experience for a young musician.

Starting in 2014, visitors with musical aspirations could sign up for five minutes of fame playing the Longwood Organ during Open Organ Console Days, generally twice a year. The morning is booked solid with five-minute performances by guests of all ages and musical abilities, assisted by a guest organist.

Capping the arts were return engagements outdoors by the Philadelphia Orchestra in 2008, after a 67-year absence, and again in 2011, 2013, and 2016. Longwood's arts mission has clearly found a new voice.

FROM TOP: Organist Rudy Lucente helps a budding musician try out the organ on Open Console Day, 2018; Philadelphia Orchestra concert in Main Fountain Garden, June 28, 2008.

OPPOSITE: More than 200 orchids on the center columns of the Exhibition Hall, with 350 orchids framing the distant Music Room windows during Orchid Extravaganza, 2018.

Special horticultural festivities matched the exuberance of performing arts. An orchid in 2006 and a camellia in 2008 were named 'Alice B. du Pont' by the respective national plant societies to honor the wife of Longwood's founder. A garden-wide site-specific *InTREEgue* art exhibit explored environmental aspects of trees at eight locations and featured Longwood's first cell-phone commentary in 2007. Farmers' giant pumpkins weighing up to 1,421 pounds apiece competed in the autumn of 2008 and 2009. Six staff visited Japan in 2008 to learn disappearing Japanese mum cultivation techniques, and Longwood's annual Chrysanthemum Festival was highlighted by a 454-bloom mum in 2008, a 718-bloom specimen in 2009, 991 blooms in 2010, 1416 blooms in 2013 (plus a 535-bloom plant transported to the US Botanic Garden on the Mall in Washington, DC), and 1523 blooms on one plant in 2016, the largest in the country. *Culinature*, an outdoor progressive dinner of regional produce, was first offered in the fall of 2008 for 100 guests seated at a 90-foot-long table outdoors in the Idea Garden. *Lilytopia*, a 10-day extravaganza of 10,000 cut stems from Dutch lily hybridizers arranged in fragrant, innovative designs, debuted in spring 2010 to national acclaim and was repeated in 2011. In 2010, Longwood opened a Student Exhibition Garden, initially funded by longtime Advisory Committee member Nancy du Pont Reynolds Cooch (1919-2015) and created by the Professional Gardener trainees to focus visitor attention on their skills; it has been redesigned each year by the succeeding class.

A vision of Van Gogh was realized in September 2010 when 22 acres of sunflowers on a perimeter field exploded with 465,000 golden flowers that attracted thousands of viewers. The field yielded 36,360 pounds of seed and was an example of Longwood sharing beauty with the community outside the garden walls.

OPPOSITE, CLOCKWISE FROM TOP LEFT: Thousand Bloom Chrysanthemum with 1,523 blooms on one plant, 2016; Student Exhibition Garden, 2010. The design changes each year to reflect Longwood's overall programmatic theme; An estimated 465,000 sunflowers in a 22-acre field west of the Conservatory, 2010. RIGHT: 14' columns of lilies during *Lilytopia*, 2010.

A Trial Garden opened within the Idea Garden in 2013 to evaluate herbaceous annuals and perennials for display potential. Guests were asked to vote for their favorites. By 2015, the emphasis moved from taxonomic groups to numerous plant combination beds designed by various staff, who labeled them with catchy titles. Dahlias were also added and greatly expanded by 2017, appropriate because Longwood is hosting the 2018 National Dahlia Show. Since voting started, more than 11,000 ballots have been cast, registering 33,000 votes for favorite plants and combinations. The Trial Garden has become a must-see bonanza of dynamic color and texture from summer through fall.

The Plant Records Office documents these miracles of nature and used the latest technology to create digital maps of the gardens in 2005 and both GPS and laser surveying equipment to continually update them. Temporary floral display crops and plants growing in natural areas were finally incorporated into the Plant Records database in 2010, so that all of Longwood's plants are now tracked. In 2013, Plant Records was moved out of the Horticulture Department and into Education's Library and Information Systems division. Longwood's herbarium of more than 15,000 pressed plant specimens was photographed then in 2018 was donated to Philadelphia's Academy of Natural Sciences of Drexel University, the oldest natural science research institution and museum in the Americas.

Most importantly, Longwood developed guidelines to help staff determine how to manage the Gardens' diverse collection of more than 11,000 taxa (types) of plants. In 2011, staff formulated a plant collection policy that was revised in 2017 to recognize 16 plant groups important to Longwood's mission. Boxwood, camellias, chrysanthemums, deciduous azaleas,

RIGHT: Trial Garden combination beds, each designed by different Outdoor Display gardeners, 2017.

magnolias, orchids, Peirce trees, waterlilies, and Victoria waterplatters are Core Collections that are intensely managed and assigned curators. Australian plants, bonsai, ferns, hollies, lilacs, oaks, and South African plants are Heritage Collections and are more loosely managed. Four Core Collections were granted Plant Collections Network accreditation by the American Public Gardens Association: waterlilies in 2012, boxwood in 2016, and Peirce's trees and chrysanthemums in 2017; more will follow. Such endorsement by this national organization recognizes that Longwood upholds and exemplifies the very best practices in the long-term care and conservation of these important collections. The Peirce collection is particularly remarkable, with 300 trees dating from the 19th century identified as still growing on the original Peirce land; probably another 50 will be discovered in the next few years, bringing the total to about 350.

The Horticulture staff also developed separate but interlacing land management plans, collectively called "Soil to Sky," for the land, turf, and trees that are establishing innovative environmental stewardship practices not only for Longwood but for public gardens everywhere. The Specimen Tree Replacement Plan is relevant to an historic property determined to preserve the heritage and aesthetic provided by mature trees and shrubs. It identifies what plants to preserve, determines how they should be replaced and, if needed, propagated, and schedules final transplanting. So far Longwood has more than 50 propagations from historic trees, and another two dozen will be propagated in the near future.

As a continuation of the naturalized bulb plantings begun in 1985, a huge team of staff, students, and volunteers spent 17,000 hours in the autumn of 2015 planting 451,000 geophytes of six species throughout the grounds, including 250,000 yellow 'Tete-a-tete' narcissi on Conifer Knoll.

In 2016, another 209,000 geophytes of six species were planted in several areas, ensuring even more rivers of color in late winter and early spring.

Reinvigoration of horticulture research and its programs has resulted in exciting initiatives that have expanded Longwood's expertise locally, nationally, and internationally. Trips to collect plants were taken to Argentina in 2006 and 2008 and to Russia and Macedonia in 2007, continuing a tradition dating back to 1956. Trips to northern Vietnam in 2014, Japan in 2016, and the American Southeast in 2017 were successful in bringing new types of plants to the Gardens for evaluation. In 2016, Longwood joined the Plant Collecting Collaborative (PCC), a group of 15 public gardens with interest in domestic and international plant collecting, and participated in trips to the Republic of Georgia in 2016 and Azerbaijan in 2017 that resulted in new plants to evaluate. This provides material for Longwood's Research Plant Trials that are a driving force behind the innovative horticulture displays seen throughout the Gardens. Longwood also adopted the most recent protocols for implementing the Convention on Biological Diversity, an international treaty designed to sustain the rich diversity of life on Earth.

As a corollary to the Plant Exploration effort, a formal Plant Conservation Program was developed in 2013 with an emphasis on US native orchid field work, seed collection, propagation research, and collection development. Working with partners in Pennsylvania, Delaware, and Virginia, staff is focusing on state-endangered and regionally rare species that are also infrequently grown in public gardens. Propagation research has been formally initiated for seven species: dragon's mouth, large yellow and Kentucky lady's slippers, two types of fringed orchids, checkered rattlesnake plantain, and Case's ladies' tresses. This work will result in the development

OPPOSITE: New plantings of 'Tete-a-tete' narcissi on Oak Knoll, 2017.

of a conservation-oriented, *ex-situ* (apart from natural habitat) collection of native orchids to be incorporated into Conservatory orchid displays, appropriate areas of the gardens proper, and the natural lands.

The plant breeding program that was established at Longwood in the late 1950s has resulted in more than 130 plant releases since that time. *Canna* and *Clivia* programs continue to produce new plants for introduction. The selection *Canna* 'Longwood Simply Salmon' was released in 2016, and five *Clivia* selections have been named: 'Longwood Debutante' (2011), 'Longwood Fireworks' (2012), 'Longwood Sunrise' (2015), 'Longwood Chimes' (2016) and 'Longwood Sunset' (2017). New breeding programs involving *Phlox, Euphorbia, Podophyllum,* and hardy orchids are being implemented and amplified. The camellia breeding program, the oldest such effort, refocused its emphasis on creating hardy plants after the severe winter of 2014-2015, which allowed proper assessment of truly cold-hardy selections in the evaluation plots. Research partnerships were also undertaken with universities around the country, and plant patenting of Longwood cultivars is under consideration.

A special horticultural honor was accorded staff members Sharon Loving and Jim Sutton, who were official judges for California's Tournament of Roses Parade in 2008 and 2018, respectively.

Education initiatives are at the heart of Longwood's mission and were reinvigorated in 2007, building on a vision proposed in 1956 which itself was based on Pierre du Pont's 1946 hope for "a school where students and others may receive instruction in the arts of horticulture and floriculture [via] lectures, exhibits, public meetings, classes and conferences...." Groundbreaking accomplishments providing exciting educational opportunities to all ages and skill levels include a school and youth program

LEFT: Longwood Summer Camp participants learn about waterlilies from Tim Jennings, 2016.

(launched 2007) that impacts about 35,000 K-12 students, teen volunteers, and Scouts each year with onsite and virtual field trips, summer camps, unguided visits, and special programs. Since 2012 Longwood has provided grants to schools who are designated by the State as Title 1. In 2017, Longwood sponsored 4,485 students from 55 local schools. Also new were live streaming of symposia (2010); realignment of resident student programs into Domestic & International Studies (2009) to parallel college standards; an annual Garden Educators' Forum (2009 to 2016) for more than 100 staff from 40 organizations; an online Plant Explorer (2010) for anyone wishing to locate and learn about Longwood's plants; and an innovative Continuing Education program of about 175 courses which resulted in more than 5,300 registrations for courses in 2017, engaging close to 2,500 individuals.

In 2009, an Online Classroom began which supports and extends the learning experience. Longwood's first free, self-paced online course, on orchids, debuted in 2018. Designed for both beginners and enthusiasts, topics ranged from the history of Longwood's collection, to proper care and breeding, to conservation of native species. Future online courses on diverse gardening topics are planned.

In 2011, Longwood's International Program was enhanced to provide intern visas in addition to trainee visas and the offerings were expanded beyond horticulture to include Education, Library and Archives, and Marketing and Public Relations. A partnership with the Garden Club of America and the Royal Horticultural Society was formed in 2011 to host the GCA/RHS Interchange Fellowship allowing for a British student to study and learn at Longwood Gardens. In 2012, a High School and Technical College Cooperative Education Program was instituted with oppor-

tunities for students from regional states (DE, MD, PA, NJ) to gain paid, hands-on, practical training complementing their school curriculum. A Bilateral Staff & Student Exchange Program that same year was implemented to provide professional development of staff and students with five peer institutions abroad in Singapore, China, and the United Kingdom. In 2013, a national Seed Your Future initiative began with the mission "To promote horticulture and inspire people to pursue careers working with plants." A ground-breaking TRIAD Fellowship started in 2014 gives students from Longwood, the National Trust (UK), and the Alliance of Hyogo (Japan) the opportunity to spend four months in each of those three countries gaining both cultural and horticultural knowledge.

In 2017, the Longwood Graduate Program, dating from 1967 in conjunction with the University of Delaware, was replaced by the Longwood Fellows Program, a 13-month residential learning experience designed for those who have a passion to lead in a public horticulture environment. The previous program educated more than 200 graduate students, many now in top management and educational positions throughout the world. The new program, based at Longwood and providing travel and internships throughout the world, has altered the focus to build leadership capacity exclusively in public horticulture. A spacious 1930 house adjoining Longwood and built by Pierre du Pont for his farm manager was re-acquired and updated to house the Fellows and their activities, as well as to host visiting faculty.

A different type of training began in 2012, when Longwood launched its Guest Experience Academy, an intensive program designed to help staff better engage with visitors and provide the steps of service that lead to an extraordinary guest experience. To date, more than 400 Longwood per-

sonnel have completed the two-day training. In 2013, Longwood began offering the Academy to colleagues from other gardens and cultural institutions. Representatives from 42 public gardens and museums have participated and more are expected.

Longwood's Library and Archives provide outstanding resources for these many educational programs and for the entire staff. The holdings include more than 35,000 library items with more than 23,000 unique titles, 6,000 ebooks, and 300 print and 3,700 online periodicals; institutional archives holding traditional and digital records as well as thousands of historic objects; and a web-based Digital Gallery (2009) of hundreds of thousands of old and new photographic images, videos, and audio files. A Community Read designed to spark discussion through a work of literature started in 2014 and has featured one adult book and titles for younger readers each year on gardens, plants, and nature in conjunction with six library systems and several cultural institutions. In 2017, the celebrated author David Macaulay spoke, and there were 120 related events over six weeks reaching as many as 5,000 readers.

Several books and DVDs were published on diverse topics. Eileen Maroney wrote *The Magic Shrub* (2006) as children's fiction set at Longwood. Tomasz Aniśko's *When Perennials Bloom* (2008) is an authoritative guide to the flowering times of 462 perennials. *Pierre S. du Pont – A Rare Genius* (2008) is a fascinating hour-long DVD about the Gardens' founder, narrated by actor Peter Coyote; a companion book (2009) was written by Michelle Ferrari. Colvin Randall's *Longwood Gardens Christmas* (2010) is the definitive history of a century of holiday celebrations. Longwood also contributed chapters to and underwrote the publication of *Public Garden Management* (2011), the first professional textbook on establishing

and maintaining viable botanical gardens and arboreta worldwide. *Light: Installations by Bruce Munro* (2012) is a 60-page photographic essay on the 2012 exhibit. *Victoria: The Seductress* by Tomasz Aniśko (2013) is the first comprehensive book chronicling the discovery, impact, and influence of the mammoth Amazonian waterplatter that is one of the world's most fascinating plants. *Longwood Gardens* (2017) by Colvin Randall for Arcadia's *Images of Modern America* series features newly discovered color photos, some more than 100 years old, to present a pictorial look back at the Gardens' unique history. In 2018, *Longwood Gardens Fountains* was published, the first on that topic since 1960.

In the summer of 2014, publication of the *Longwood Chimes* resumed with Issue #289. The series began in 1957 as an in-house newsletter for staff, but it has been reimagined as an artful, twice-a-year Member and staff journal that explores the best that Longwood offers, with in-depth articles and imaginative photography.

Pulling Out All The Stops (2015) is a DVD that documents Longwood's 2013 International Organ Competition, with in-depth looks at the ten contestants leading up to the awarding of prizes. *Longwood Gardens: A Personal Tour* (2016) is an hour-long DVD that visits more than 50 garden areas, as guided by Colvin Randall. *Flowing Water* (2017) is a DVD documentary that chronicles the rebirth of Longwood's Main Fountain Garden. Both fountain and organ films were broadcast several times on selected TV stations across the nation. Three CDs of organ music were produced since the organ renovation, plus a CD compilation of Firmin Swinnen's historic recordings, bringing the total to about 36 organ, carillon, piano, or vocal recordings released as records, tapes, or CDs since the 1950s.

OPPOSITE: Late April and early May along the Flower Garden Walk, with dogwood, tulips, and many other springtime blooms, 2011.

Volunteers have made a huge impact on the institution. From one volunteer in 1989 to more than 800 today, the program is one of Longwood's great success stories. Behind the scenes, volunteers conduct research, propagate plants, and maintain plant records. In the gardens, they plant, prune, and fine tune the appearance of both formal and natural areas. Volunteer-led wildflower and bird walks engage guests and raise awareness of the significance of Longwood's natural lands. The last 10 years have seen a rapid growth in volunteer roles that enhance guests' experiences, including through six Interpretive Docent teams and four Garden Ambassador teams. From crafting Christmas ornaments and evaluating trees, to capturing photographic images or explaining the organ, to planting thousands of bulbs and maintaining 200 bluebird nest boxes, volunteers support Longwood in extraordinary ways.

Vast amounts of both contractual and staff labor were required for major construction projects completed over the last decade. Longwood's main entrance gates, originally installed in 1964, were enlarged in August 2005 with revised traffic patterns and new welcome signs. In late 2009, tall evergreens were planted just inside to screen the grassy overflow parking lot, and the gates were relandscaped in 2010 and more signs added, creating a new look to greet arriving guests.

In 2006, a state-of-the-art Archives facility opened with protected storage for thousands of historic documents, images, recordings, and artifacts, and for priceless horticultural books and periodicals.

The indoor Garden Path along the southern edge of the East Conservatory reopened in early 2007, followed in October by the adjoining Children's Garden, which had been originally designed in 1987 and remade in

FROM TOP: Children's Garden Central Cove with fantasy sculptures shooting rod-like water jets into pool below, 2007; Children's Garden Drooling Dragon in Secret Room inspired by Bomarzo, the famous Italian "monster" garden, 2007. OPPOSITE, FROM TOP: Children's Garden Square Maze and arched Apse with cross-firing laminar flow water jets, 2009; Children's Garden concept drawing by lead designer Tres Fromme, 1999.

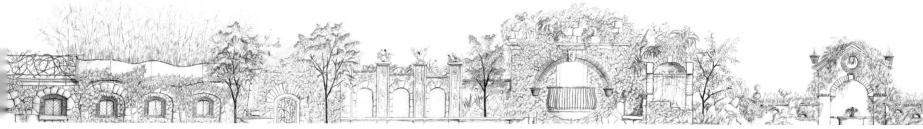

1990. In 1997, Tres Fromme and Mary Allinson visited other children's gardens, zoos, and museums and worked with youngsters to define how the newest Longwood version imparts the joys of a pleasure garden. Fromme's design created a Central Cove, Secret Room, Ramp, Grotto Cave, and Bamboo Maze embellished by whimsical sculptures, jewel-like mosaics, and leaping, drooling, and misty fountains that quickly became treasured friends for young visitors.

In 2009 and 2018, the Terrace Restaurant was given major interior makeovers. Hugely popular with guests has been an annual Beer Garden outdoors during summers since 2015, with signature brews, a comfort menu, and often live music. Huge attendance increases have made it necessary to erect tented structures to accommodate the restaurant overflow.

In October 2009, the Gardens' total acreage increased with the purchase of 19 acres adjoining the northern perimeter, and in 2017 with an additional six, also to the north, for a total of 1,083 acres. The property extends Longwood's surrounding green buffer, preserves the agrarian landscape, and provides a location for support services.

A major milestone was the completion of the outdoor East Conservatory Plaza. A design had been under discussion since 2000 when it was proposed that a formal plaza outside the East could connect with a replacement restaurant to be built north of the existing one. But eventually that concept was discarded, and in 2007 British landscape architect Kim Wilkie was engaged to come up with a simpler solution. With a few dramatic brush strokes, Wilkie conceived of a crisp, bold landform reminiscent of the sweeping grass terraces of such 18th-century English landscapes as Claremont and Studley Royal, or Middleton Place in South Carolina. The curved turf steps (which are cut using a small hover mower)

RIGHT: Beer Garden outside Terrace Restaurant, October 2016

are backed by a hill to the north to mask a long but narrow glass-roofed spine housing 17 domed, naturally lit lavatory cabinets hidden within. Indoors, the central corridor which connects to the East Conservatory is walled on both sides with a 3,590-square-foot vertical garden with 25 species of mostly ferns, totaling 47,000 plants, at the time the largest Green Wall in North America. The area is so cleverly concealed that first-time visitors usually miss it unless directed there. Construction began in the fall of 2009, and the $11.4 million project officially opened in October 2010. In 2014, an online nationwide contest named the facility the best public restroom in the country!

Away from the core gardens were two major projects that helped preserve the natural environment. First, in 2011 Longwood turned to "green" energy, purchasing power only from hydro-electric but now instead from wind-energy sources and, most importantly, from an onsite $7 million, nine-acre solar field with 6,682 solar panels that generate approximately two million kilowatt hours annually to reduce mid-day demand on the energy grid by more than 50%. This first phase was partially funded by the State's PA Green Energy Works program. As of 2018, Longwood continues to actively evaluate solar projects for cost-effective opportunities.

A second major improvement was the straightening and relocation of Route 52 that bisected the Gardens between U.S. Route 1 and Route 926. After 20 years of discussion and a $3.5 million Longwood-funded design, the $18.7 million state-funded project improved public safety and made more Longwood land available for visitor use. The road opened in 2011. Although 10 acres of trees had to be removed, 22 acres of new

OPPOSITE: East Plaza seen from above, 2010. The sweeping grass terraces cover 13,800 square feet, and the indoor Green Wall is hidden beneath the curving glass roof in upper left half of the photo. RIGHT, FROM TOP: Curving Green Wall with 47,000 plants creates a vertical garden around 17 lavatory cabinets, 2011; Hover mower that floats on a cushion of air, 2010.

forest were planted. Restoration of the Pocopson Stream wetland that flows through the property and into the Brandywine was an important aspect of the project.

Guest parking had become a problem in recent years, particularly at Christmas when satellite lots more than a mile away were used. Finally, for

Christmas 2016 a new lot on the south side of Route 1 near Longwood's nursery and solar field was finished, with 1,170 paved spaces, almost as large as the 1,302-car Visitor Center lot. Shuttle buses transport guests to the Visitor Center efficiently. That winter, the GardenShop in the Visitor Center was redesigned to its largest size ever.

FROM LEFT: Some of the 6,682 solar panels in Longwood's solar field south of Route One, 2011; Solar Flower in the Idea Garden tracks the sun under its own power, 2012. OPPOSITE: Main Fountain Garden reconstruction showing future underground

Upper Canal reservoir and pump room. In the distance, the Rectangular Basin pump room is being carved out of the hillside behind the remnants of the soon-to-be-rebuilt arched fountain wall, June 2015.

But the biggest project of all was rebuilding the Main Fountain Garden. Discussion began in 1991, but it was not until 2012 that detailed planning was underway, following completion of the 2011 Master Plan. Beyer Blinder Belle from New York was chosen to head the revitalization, having worked on Grand Central Terminal, Ellis Island, the US Capitol, and Lincoln Center's Promenade. Fluidity Design Consultants from Los Angeles designed Longwood's new hydraulics and West 8 the landscape, along with L'Observatoire International for site lighting. Construction began in late 2014, adding 1,400 feet of new tunnels to provide access to all utilities, plumbing, and wiring, unlike the old garden where these critical arteries were buried directly in the soil. To provide pumphouse temperature and humidity control, 30 geothermal wells were drilled into the Picnic Area parking lot and connected with buried pipes.

All the legacy fountain effects were retained, but with new height control. The old central 130-foot jet can now zoom up to 175 feet. Sixteen five-stream spinning nozzles were added, along with eight nozzles that can move side to side and 11 nozzles that can move in any direction. In the Canals, circular pipes with 40 small jets apiece give a unique basketweave

effect to the 29 stone octagon enclosures, totaling 1,200 new nozzles. The icing on the fountain cake is 32 air-propelled water "cannons" that blast 100 feet high with a controllable soft pop to loud bang. Competing for the surprise factor are 30 flame jets that appear like aquatic birthday candles atop the Upper and Lower Canal jets. The old garden had 386 jets, sprays, scuppers, spouts, waterfalls, and weirs; the new garden has 1,719.

There are 68 display and filtration pumps (compared to 15 used in the old garden) in four pump rooms. The maximum recirculation rate is about 40,000 gallons per minute, compared with 10,000 gpm for the old system.

An astounding conservation effort was undertaken to preserve the historic stonework that had been carved for Mr. du Pont in Italy and Philadelphia in the 1930s. Dan Lepore & Sons Company from Conshohocken, PA, brought in 25 masons in 2014 to dismantle 5,312 pieces of stone. In all, 4,457 pieces of Italian and Indiana limestone were restored, 855 pieces were created to replace those beyond repair, and 61 pieces of serpentine and marble were restored or replaced, adding up to 5,373 pieces. Some of the replacements were carved from the same vein of Italian limestone as the original work. In total, the stonework took more than 68,000 hours to complete. It was inspected with enthusiasm by Barbara Morseletto, granddaughter of the original Italian designer and carver Pietro Morseletto (1887-1974), at a gala inaugural event in May 2017.

Architectural changes included a new stairway at the southeastern corner to allow easier access to the upper level. At the southwestern corner, the old balustrade stairs were replaced with an arcaded extension that mimics the arched Pumphouse Façade yet allows easy passage through to a new Pumphouse Plaza to the south and to the Rectangular Basin above via a monumental staircase with an elevator.

ABOVE, FROM TOP: 168 'Greenspire' lindens wrap the Main Fountain Garden in a giant U-shaped allée, providing a shady retreat from which to enjoy the flowing water; At dusk, the garden is magically lit with more than 1,700 LED fixtures, 2017.

OPPOSITE: Flames erupt and travel up the canal jets to form aquatic torches at dramatic musical points in an evening fountain show, 2017.

But the most exciting architectural feature was a new Grotto hidden behind the restored Loggia in the center of the Pumphouse Façade wall. Seventy tons of stone form a dome room encircling a round water curtain pouring from a ceiling oculus. On the south side 20 more tons are stacked into a planted panoramic wall lit from above. The Grotto was the work of Gary Odle from Stonescapes, Inc., of Landenberg, PA.

Outdoors, the garden from the Conservatory Terrace looks very much like the original. A large paved esplanade fronts the Reception Suite, usually dotted with tubbed boxwood. A U-shaped linden allée of 168 *Tilia cordata* 'Greenspire' replaced the original Norway maples that are now known to be invasive. A monumental planting of boxwood delineates the canals with green "eye-liner." The 3,000 *Buxus microphylla* var. *japonica* 'Green Beauty' are pruned in a free-flowing hybrid approach that is both contrived yet organic.

Walking down into the garden reveals more obvious changes, especially in the replacement of turf and ground cover with decomposed granite, known as DG. The allées now resemble a Parisian park such as the Tuileries with large expanses of DG under trimmed trees and peppered with benches for much freer and random access. The redesigned landscape was expanded to include new designs and plantings for the former Caryopteris Allée to the east and the Hillside Garden to the south.

It is at night when the extraordinary magic of the garden is readily visible. More than 1,700 LED fixtures cast a warm white glow on the paths, wall fountains, and stonework. The 29 limestone octagons in the canals have white LEDs uplighting the external carvings for the first time. The overall effect is like strolling through Rome after dark. And then the show fountains erupt in a saturated rainbow of ever-so-intense color. The

LEFT: The restored Loggia and Fountain Wall, of carved Italian and plain Indiana limestone, are worthy of a Renaissance villa garden, 2017. OPPOSITE: The new Grotto's 90 tons of stone with a circular water curtain create a mysterious chamber buried in the hillside, 2017.

new 1,005 color fixtures are each filled with red, blue, green, amber, cyan, and lime LED diodes. The system was developed for Longwood by Crystal Fountains of Toronto. An additional 19 moving fixtures encircle the robotic nozzles and have red, blue, and green LEDs. Together, these 1,024 fixtures permit millions of colors at many times the old saturation.

A German-made computer program called Syncronorm Depence handles the 8,192 channels needed to control the fountains. It has a visualizer that allows the programmer to see a realistic color video of a show during the design process. The show can be tweaked repeatedly and the results are immediately visible prior to actually running the fountains on site.

A new state-of-the-art sound system surrounds the audience with music coming from the front as well as from behind. Portable speaker towers add even more definition for fireworks displays.

The old technology has not been forgotten, however. The historic Pumphouse with its 1930s equipment was transformed into a permanent museum exhibit, with descriptions of how it all worked originally. A temporary exhibit in the Conservatory Music Room during the summer of 2017 told how fountain shows and fireworks have embellished Longwood for decades to the delight of millions.

The Main Fountain Garden Revitalization was truly an international effort, with 94 suppliers from at least 13 US states, Canada, United Kingdom, France, Germany, and Italy. All this expertise was costly at $90 million for the fountains, plus several million more for a new electric substation that can handle future needs for all of Longwood. But it was all worth it. During the initial 2017 fountain season, more than 732,000 guests were dazzled by both daytime and evening displays that showed

OPPOSITE: The Upper Canal at dusk features illuminated jets and glowing stonework, 2017. ABOVE: The Main Fountain Garden at full capacity thrusts jets up to 175' skyward, 2017.

off the full range of fountain effects accompanied by all types of music. The project also initiated a new era of sophisticated 21st-century Facilities management, with the substation and Main Fountain Garden as the hub from which infrastructure can develop and grow.

The future of Longwood is both bright and challenging. Attendance reached a record high of more than 1.55 million visitors for 2017, almost double from just a decade earlier. Half the visits were by Members, reflecting a huge increase in loyal stakeholders. In 1973, Longwood first offered an Annual Neighbor Pass that was eventually renamed the Frequent Visitor Pass. Although participants always considered themselves "members," it wasn't until 2007 that the program took on benefits like those offered at other cultural institutions. Finally, in 2010 the title Member was adopted, with enhancements added in 2017. The results have been astounding. From 11,000 individuals in 1992 and 16,000 households in 2007, by 2011 the total rose to 38,000 households comprising 97,000 adults and children. By 2017, there were 67,000 Member households, totaling 193,000 individuals, each household on average visiting 12 times per year.

Greater attendance can lead to crowding, especially at Christmas, so timed tickets offered online were first tried for the 2008 holidays. These permitted guests to avoid ticketing lines and allowed Longwood to limit the total number of visitors in the Gardens. Visitors and Longwood increasingly communicate with each other online for everything from ticketing and registrations to course work and interpretation as internet technology, smartphone usage, and social media (first used in 2009) become essential gateways to building Longwood's brand and expanding the guest experience. Currently about 320,000 people engage with Longwood on social media channels every day; 32,000 guests provide valuable feedback each year through online surveys; and the Gardens' website receives more than 11 million page views annually.

The future challenges are significant. Budgeted operating expenses are nearly $60 million a year, with capital expenditures adding as much

OPPOSITE: The wide Half-Round Fan in the Lower Canal mimics even larger fans in the Rectangular Basin behind, 2017. ABOVE: Both spinning jets and explosive water cannons are new additions to the distant Rectangular Basin, 2017.

as $40 million more per year when major projects are underway. Despite these impressive totals, Longwood does not actively fundraise. By living within existing resources and growing its attendance and revenue through an innovative entrepreneurial spirit, Longwood is able to currently cover 62% of the operating budget from earned revenue, which reinforces the ability to survive in perpetuity regardless of the economic climate.

The staff of 1,700 employees, students, and volunteers is inspired by a newly redefined shared vision built on that conceived by Pierre S. du Pont. Facility maintenance never ceases. Energy issues are critical. Advancing excellence in garden design, horticulture, education, and the arts is paramount. In a world where technology and communications have seemingly accelerated daily life, having a culture of planning at all levels ensures that Longwood stays on target and has a future. Today's audiences have been everywhere and have done everything, much more so than in past decades. The authenticity of Longwood must be preserved if the Gardens are to sus-

tain a healthy dynamic and remain relevant. The public recognizes when something is uniquely special, so the perception of Longwood as the very best takes top priority.

For decades Longwood Gardens has been a revered horticultural display, but recent growth of programs, attendance, budget, and accomplishments have pushed it into the forefront of American cultural institutions. What will there be to celebrate in 2106? Impossible to know, but one hopes for universal acclaim that recognizes Longwood as a garden of unparalleled ambition and diverse experiences.

ABOVE, FROM LEFT: 1,400' of underground tunnels give unprecedented access to all utilities of the Main Fountain Garden, 2016; The original Pump Room is now a permanent museum exhibit giving a close-up look at the technology of the 1931 installation, 2017. OPPOSITE: A Fireworks and Fountain display is a multi-sensory spectacle that has to be seen to be believed. Notice the flames atop the Canal jets, 2017.

SPRING AT LONGWOOD

CLOCKWISE, FROM TOP LEFT: In Conservatory, 2009; Along Flower Garden Walk, 2010; In Idea Garden, 2010; Around Square Fountain, 2010.

SUMMER AT LONGWOOD

CLOCKWISE, FROM TOP LEFT: Waterlilies at dusk, 2017; Water flume in Hillside Garden, 2008; Summer fireworks, 2008; Orangery, 2009.

AUTUMN AT LONGWOOD

CLOCKWISE FROM TOP LEFT: Chrysanthemums in Orangery, 2009; Round Fountain on Flower Garden Walk, 2009; Fall color at Large Lake, 2010; Spiral mum topiaries in Exhibition Hall, 2010; Meadow Garden sunset, 2014.

WINTER AT LONGWOOD

CLOCKWISE, FROM TOP: Fountain of Lights, 2013; Love Temple by Large Lake, 2008; Lighted trees in and around Large Lake, 2017.

CHRISTMAS AT LONGWOOD

CLOCKWISE FROM LEFT: East Conservatory, 2010; Exhibition Hall, 2011; Exhibition Hall with floating tapestry of 18,540 red and green apples, 2013; Exhibition Hall 64' table set for a floral feast, 2012.

CLOCKWISE FROM TOP: Christmas at Longwood, Exhibition Hall swan, 2014; Exhibition Hall poinsettia tree, 2016; Music Room, 2017; Exhibition Hall 8,000 green apples, 670,000 cranberries, and 3,000 walnuts floating parterre, 2017; Exhibition Hall poinsettia trees, 2015; Exhibition Hall cream-colored poinsettias, 2010.

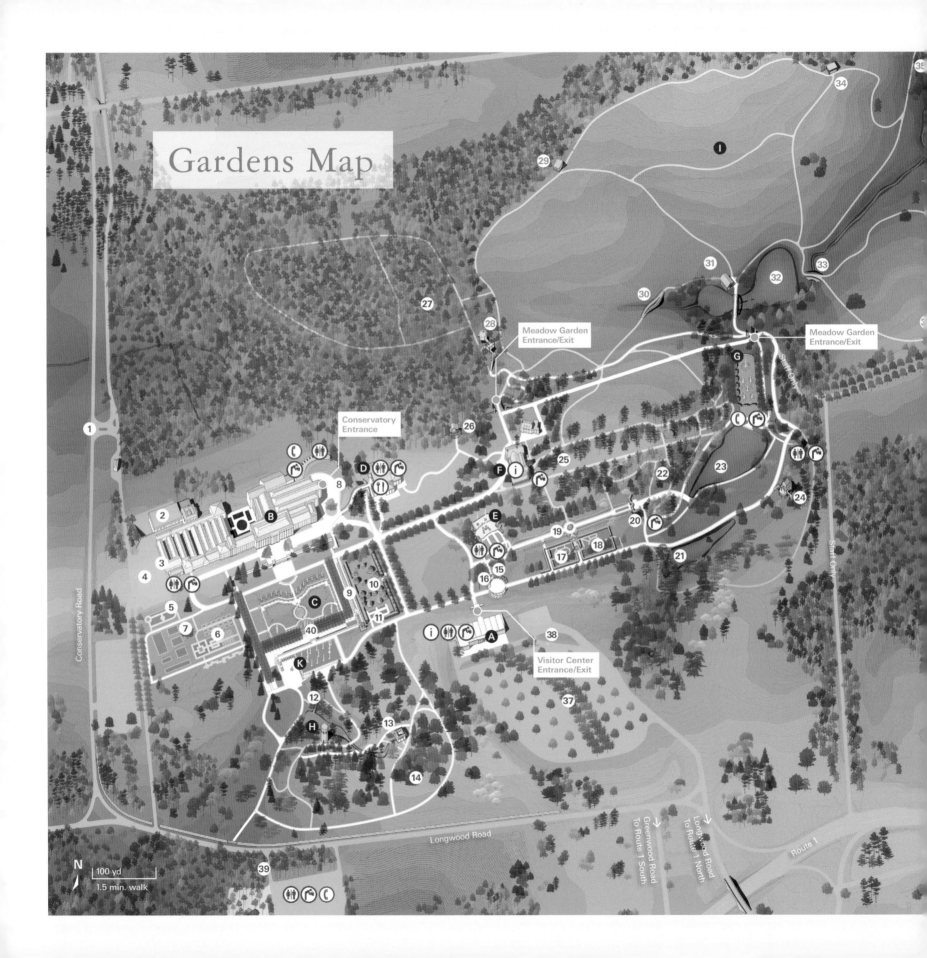

Gardens Map

Conservatory Entrance

Meadow Garden Entrance/Exit

Meadow Garden Entrance/Exit

Visitor Center Entrance/Exit

Conservatory Road

Longwood Road

Greenwood Road
To Route 1 South

Longwood Road
To Route 1 North

Route 1

N

100 yd
1.5 min. walk

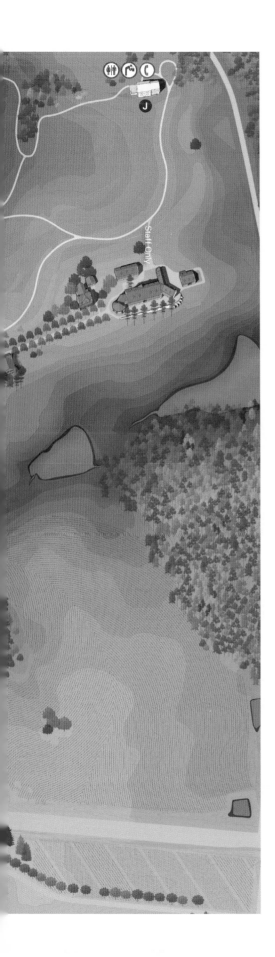

GARDEN FEATURES

A Visitor Center and The GardenShop

B Conservatory

C Main Fountain Garden

D The Terrace: The Café, 1906

E Open Air Theatre

F Peirce-du Pont House

G Italian Water Garden

H Chimes Tower

I Meadow Garden

J Webb Farmhouse & Galleries

K Historic Pump Room and Gallery

1 Business Entrance

2 Offices/Betula, Acer Classrooms

3 Catalpa Classroom

4 Employee Parking

5 Student Exhibition Garden

6 Idea Garden/Trial Garden

7 Children's Corner

8 East Conservatory Plaza

9 Carpinus Allée

10 Topiary Garden

11 Rose Garden

12 Hillside Garden

13 Eye of Water

14 Oak and Conifer Knoll

15 Theatre Garden

16 Rose Arbor

17 Peony Garden

18 Wisteria Garden

19 Flower Garden Walk

20 Whispering Bench

21 Small Lake

22 Peirce's Woods

23 Large Lake

24 Canopy Cathedral Treehouse

25 Peirce's Park

26 Birdhouse Treehouse

27 Forest Walk

28 Lookout Loft Treehouse

29 Forest Edge

30 Meadow Bridge

31 Hourglass Lake Pavilion

32 Hourglass Lake

33 Earth Bridge

34 Pollinator Overlook

35 Beech Forest Boardwalk

36 Hawk Point

37 Guest Parking

38 Bus Parking

39 Picnic Area

40 The Grotto

Public Restrooms

Drinking Fountain

Dining

Emergency Phone

Elevators

Stairs

Information

Wheelchair Accessible

Gardens are Smoke-free

Ownership & Management

CONSULTING LANDSCAPE ARCHITECTS

Church, Thomas 1971–1977

Shepheard, Sir Peter...........................1977–2002

Reed Hilderbrand LLC... 2002–2006, 2018–Present

West 8.. 2009–Present

CONSULTING ARCHITECTS AND ENGINEERS

Bancroft Construction Company.... 2008–Present

Weiss/Manfredi 2009–Present

Beyer Blinder Belle...........................2012–2017

MANAGEMENT STAFF

DIRECTOR (renamed President & CEO in 2016)

Seibert, Russell J. 1955–1979

Miller, Everitt L. 1979–1984
  Assistant Director 1963–1979

Roberts, Frederick E. 1984–2006

Redman, Paul B. 2006–Present

FARM

Baily, Joseph......................................1906–1912

Farquhar, Malcolm 1912–1929

Gilpin, Douglas................................1929–1951
  Tree Nursery Manager 1952–1965

CONSTRUCTION

Francis, William L. 1908–1924

Taylor, Roland 1911–1949

HORTICULTURE

Hannum, Henry 1910–1915
  (flowers)

Alexander, Ambrose 1911–1933
  (vegetables)

Mulliss, William 1916–1945

Marx, John H. 1945–1959

Miller, Everitt L. 1959–1979

Carstens, F. Joseph............................1979–1990

Edmonds, C. Ross, Jr. 1990–1996

Stites, Jerry S. 1997–2004

Loving, Sharon 2004–Present

MAINTENANCE (renamed Facilities in 2010)

Brewer, Russell P. 1920–1960

Bowen, Knowles R. 1960–1965

Jarvela, Arthur L. 1965–1985

Meyn, Charles 1985–1990

Stozek, Robert L. 1990–1999

Underwood, Robert W. 1999–2008

Winnicki, Mark P. 2009–2013

Kenneth, Grablewski.................... 2014–Present

ADMINISTRATION

Thompson, George E., Sr. 1954–1971

Thompson, George E. Jr. 1971–1989

Thompson, Alton K. 1989–1998
  Assistant Director 1989–1998

Taunk, Kiran 1998–2001

Fisher, Dennis R. 2002–Present

EDUCATION

Hodge, Walter H. 1955–1961

Paul, Lois W. 1963–1975

Apps, Darrel A. 1975–1987

Thomas, R. William..........................1987–1999

O'Leary, Susan M. 1999–2001

Gestram, Iris 2001–2006

Needham, Douglas C. 2007–2017

Cathcart, Sarah 2017–Present

GUEST SERVICES

McCaw, Constance S. 2007–2015

Benevento, Christopher 2016–Present

MARKETING AND COMMUNICATIONS

Shearer, Amy C. 2007–2009

Conley, Marnie P. 2009–Present

LONGWOOD GRADUATE PROGRAM COORDINATORS IN CONJUNCTION WITH THE UNIVERSITY OF DELAWARE

Lighty, Richard W.............................1967–1984

Swasey, James E. 1984–2005

Lyons, Robert E. 2005–2014

Trader, Brian 2014–2017
  Interim Director

Conley, Marnie P. 2014–2017
  Interim Co–Lead

LONGWOOD FELLOWS PROGRAM

Fleming, Tamara 2016–Present

VISITING COMMITTEE

Kimnach, Myron 1973–1975
Huntington Botanical Gardens

Lewis, Clarence............................... 1973 (1 year)
Michigan State University

Northrop, G. Harold 1973–1978
Callaway Gardens

Norweb, R. Henry, Jr. 1973–1979
Holden Arboretum

Peck, Kenneth....................................1973–1974
Missouri Botanical Garden

Schroeder, Charles R. 1973–1976
San Diego Zoo

Short, James R. 1974–1980
Colonial Williamsburg Foundation

Scholtz, Elizabeth..............................1975–1981
Brooklyn Botanic Garden

de Vos, Francis...................................1976–1982
University of Minnesota Landscape Arboretum

Ching, Francis...................................1978–1983
Los Angeles State & County Arboretum

Ballard, Ernesta D. 1979–1984
Pennsylvania Horticultural Society

Goudy, W. David...............................1981–1987
Montshire Museum

Hall, Marion.....................................1981–1987
Holden Arboretum

Eltzroth, Thomas E. 1982–1990
California Polytechnic State University

Brown, Peter A.G. 1983–1991
Colonial Williamsburg Foundation

Simmons, John.................................. 1984-1991
Royal Botanic Gardens, Kew

Frowine, Steven A. 1986–1992
W. Atlee Burpee Company

Pepper, Jane G. 1987–1994
Pennsylvania Horticultural Society

Barrick, William F. 1988–1993
Callaway Gardens

Paine, C. W. Eliot..............................1990–1997
Holden Arboretum

Henry, Lawrence................................1991–1998
Colonial Williamsburg Foundation

Zuk, Judith D. 1992–1999
Brooklyn Botanic Garden

Flint, Harrison L. 1993–2001
Purdue University

George, Alberta Sebolt 1995–2002
Old Sturbridge Village

Briggs, George 1997–2003
North Carolina Arboretum

Floyd, John Alex, Jr. 1998–2004
Southern Living Magazine

Tschanz, Eric N. 1999–2006
Powell Gardens

Archabal, Nina M. 2001–2007
Minnesota Historical Society

Bridgen, Mark P. 2002–2008
Cornell University

Sawyers, Claire E. 2003–2009
Scott Arboretum of Swarthmore College

Folsom, James P. 2004–2011
Huntington Botanical Gardens

Shimizu, Holly 2006–2012
United States Botanic Garden

Dole, John..2007–2013
North Carolina State University

Mabberly, David J. 2008–2014
Royal Botanic Gardens, Kew

Socolofsky, Kathleen.........................2009–2015
University of California Davis Arboretum

Carvallo, Henri..................................2010–2017
Chateau & Jardins de Villandry

Markert, Kate....................................2011–2018
Hillwood Estate, Museums & Gardens

Chapman, Grace 2013–2019
Lewis Ginter Botanical Garden

Bailey, Douglas..................................2014–2020
College of Agriculture and Environmental Sciences, University of Georgia

Charrington, Heather Clark...............2016–2022
English National Ballet

ABOVE: Main Fountain Garden from above, looking north, 2017.

ABOVE: Anemone in Garden Path, March 2013.

Credits

Copyright © 2005; final chapter © 2018 Longwood Gardens, Inc.
Third Edition 2018

Hardcover ISBN: 978-1-4276-0259-6

Written by Colvin Randall

Photographs by Larry Albee, Bancroft Construction Company, Kirk Brown, Hank Davis, Carol DeGuiseppi, Richard Donham, Duane Erdmann, Bob Fiori, Kelly Giarrocco, Gottscho-Schleisner, Gottlieb Hampfler, Bill Hill, Richard Keen, Emerson Marine, Becca Mathias, Rondel Peirson, Colvin Randall, Kevin Ritchie, Mary Rinderle Smith, Eileen Tercha, Jeffrey Totaro, Daniel Traub, and Deborah Webb

Historical photos from the collections of Chester County Historical Society, West Chester PA; Franklin & Marshall College, Lancaster PA; Hagley Museum and Library, Wilmington DE; David and Robert Highfield; Historical Society of Pennsylvania, Philadelphia PA; and Longwood Gardens

Designed by Susan Van Horn

Produced by Dai Nippon Printing Co., Ltd.
Printed in Malaysia

Published and distributed by
Longwood Gardens, Inc.
PO Box 501
Kennett Square, Pennsylvania 19348-0501
USA

Telephone 610-388-1000

www.longwoodgardens.org